MW00917811

# The Crowdfunding Myth

*Legally and effectively
raise money for your business*

Jillian Sidoti, Esq.

Copyright © 2016 Jillian Sidoti

All rights reserved.

ISBN: 153023722X
ISBN-13: 978-1530237227

## DEDICATION

To my husband, Derek and my three children Tyler, Tommy, and Nik. Love you all.

And to Maggie Faralli.

# CONTENTS

# ACKNOWLEDGMENTS

Special thanks to Gene Trowbridge, my partner at SyndicationLawyers.com for his encouragement during this process.

Thanks so much to the following companies and people for their amazing contributions to this book!

Craig Denlinger, CPA
Managing Partner | Attest Services
Crowdfund CPA
*Affiliate of Artesian CPA, LLC*
Office: 303.823.3220
1624 Market Street, Suite 202
Denver, CO 80202
Email: craig@crowdfundcpa.com |
www.CrowdfundCPA.com

Jay Goth
26442 Beckman Court
Murrieta CA 92562
Direct: 951.676.6509
jgoth@insocalconnect.org
www.insocalconnect.org

Amy Wan | General Counsel
Patch of Land
amy@patchofland.com
Main: (888) 959-1465
https://patchofland.com
1964 Westwood Blvd, Ste 350
Los Angeles, CA 90025

Ruth E. Hedges CEO
CrowdfundingRoadmap Inc
Thegccworld.com
Crowdfundingroadmap@gmail.com

Jennifer Gatewood, PMP
Founder
Peer Elevate & Peer Elevate Funding
jgatewood@PeerElevate.com
Office: 1-601-208-0082
Cell: 1-601-506-2061
www.PeerElevate.com
www.PeerElevateFunding.com (Mississippi's First
Equity Crowdfunding Portal!)
jgatewood@PeerElevateFunding.com

Ian Formigle
VP of Investments
CrowdStreet, Inc.
506 SW 6th Avenue #802, Portland, OR 97204
503.621.2259
crowdstreet.com

Scott Purcell | scott@fundamerica.com |
FundAmerica | 641 Lexington Avenue, Suite
1518 | New York, NY 10022
Fundamerica.com

Melinda Moore
Moore Media Ventures
melinda@melindamoore.com
310-339-1681

Robert Gerrard
Finaeos
robert.gerrard@finaeos.com

214-837-041
finaeos.com

Scott Whaley
NationalREIA & REIFA "Real Estate Investors
Funding Association"
Scott@REIFA.org
619-665-3543
REIFA.org

Justin Belleme
JB Media Group
justin@jbmediagroupllc.com
828-273-1280
Jbmediagroupllc.com

David Drake
LDJ Capital Family Office
Founder of the U.S. Crowd Fund Professional
Association & CFIRA

Henry S. Chavez  |  Senior Audit Manager
2300 Contra Costa Blvd, Suite 425, Pleasant Hill,
CA 94523
G: (925)  977-4000   |   D: (925)  949-5697   |
F: (866) 451-5031  |  henry@spiegelcorp.com

Thank you to Lynn Ivers Walder for  her
thoughts, opinions, and enthusiasm for
crowdfunding! You,  my friend, are one of the
many people that are going to make this brave
new world successful.

# FOREWORD

*By: Ryan Stewman, the Hardcore Closer*

I always say "you can't fake skill" and this book proves it. Many of us have wondered how the whole crowdfunding thing works. We see pages like gofundme, on a daily basis. I thought those crowdfunding sites were only for sick loved ones and funerals of the deceased. True story.

Not until working with Jillian, helping her write this book, did I realize you can use crowdfunding for so much more. It's not just limited to funerals and hospital bills. You can fund a business, a product or even an empire using micro promises from people you don't even know.

Think about all those gofundme pages you see on Facebook, that have only a couple hundred dollars pledged. Think about the business ventures who have no idea how to raise money, who fail to do so via crowdfunding too. We've all seen them.

Just like anything else, you've got to know what you're doing, in order to get sh!t done. The goal of this book is to inform you of all the ins and outs of raising money via crowd funding. Just because you put a page up with nice words and friendly pics, asking for money, doesn't mean it will work. Matter of fact, there's a higher probability that it won't work.

This book will help even those odds out for you. The experts who've been interviewed in here, are all knowledgeable and have made their priceless insight as available as an open book. The author has poured her education, head and heart into this book, in order to help people like you, avoid the pitfalls of crowdfunding.

Here's the thing: Reading this book is cool and all, but if you want any value from it, you're going to need to put what you learn, into action. This book is the blueprint to help you get paid and avoid pain, use it, live by it, get funded from it.

# I.   THE CROWDFUNDING
   MYTH DEFINED

*"A myth is an image in terms of which we try to make
sense of the world."*
Alan Watts

Recently, I was asked to give a presentation at
an entrepreneur's group here in Southern
California. The host wanted me to present for 30
minutes on how to raise private money for a small
business. I entitled the presentation *The
Crowdfunding Myth: How to Legally and Effectively Raise
Money for Your Business.* As soon as I put the first
slide up with the title in it, a gentleman in the
front row asked me, "Are you only going to speak
about crowdfunding? Because I was hoping I
could raise private money for my business."

I laughed a little bit, smiled sweetly, and said, "Well, crowdfunding is part of raising money for your business and I'm going to talk about all of the myths surrounding crowdfunding."

That was the first myth; that crowdfunding was "something else." Crowdfunding is a lot of things, including raising private money for your business. Quite frankly, crowdfunding, in the most legal sense of the term is not even fully legal yet and isn't even expected to be legal until around April or May of 2016. We're going to talk about that in the second part of this book under "Regulation CF."

There are really three different types of crowdfunding. The first type is the charitable donation crowdfunding. These are sites like GoFundMe, where someone gives money with no expectation of anything in return. This is the only type of crowdfunding that we will not be talking about in this book. So if you're looking to start an effective GoFundMe campaign, I will be honest and tell you right now that this book is not for you.

The second type of crowdfunding campaign is also on a donor model but there's usually something given in return. For example, sites like Indiegogo, PledgeMusic and Kickstarter all have a donor model. However, in exchange for your donation, you usually receive either the product or some other item in return. There is no return, like profits or interest, on the investment. We will talk about these types of crowdfunding campaigns and how to have an effective one, but that will not be the crux of this book.

The crux of this book will lie strictly in those crowdfunding opportunities that provide or promise to provide some kind of return on investment for the investor. These are the types of campaigns that we will find on websites like StartEngine, EquityNet, Wefunder, Patch of Land, CrowdStreet, Crowdfunder, CollectiveSun, Finaeos, Fundrise, Realty Shares or any of the dozens or so crowdfunding sites that offer returns on investments. We will discuss the different laws and how these sites raise money within the law. We will even discuss how to start crowdfunding from your OWN website. So if you're looking to raise money for your business and you've always wondered what crowdfunding really means, then this is the book for you.

Another myth surrounding crowdfunding is that you can go out and just start raising money without any regard to securities law. This is simply not true. Ever since the JOBS Act passed in 2012, there have been major misconceptions about how the law really works surrounding the raising of capital through crowdfunding. I really want to encourage you to read this entire book and then when you're done reading the book, keep it. It's a great reference tool for figuring out how to crowd fund your business in the future. You're not going to remember all of the laws. You're simply not. You have too many other things going on if you're an entrepreneur, to become an attorney on the side as well. So please, I encourage you to keep this book. If you know somebody else who needs it, have them buy it. Yeah, that's just me trying to sell more books. But no, seriously, have them buy the book themselves because it is a great reference material.

That is not to say you can do this alone. You are going to need a great team to effectively crowd fund your deal or your business. First, you're going to need an attorney, specifically a securities attorney. A securities attorney will help you navigate the laws and make sure that you don't violate them. They will also help you provide the proper disclosure to your investors, so that they understand what it is that they're investing in and what they can expect in return for their investment.

Second, you're going to need a great auditor or a great accountant for your company, so that the accounting for your investors is done properly.

Third, if you're really interested in crowdfunding your company or deal, you need to have a relationship with a proper crowdfunding portal or your need to build your own website from which to crowdfund. Not all crowdfunding portals are created equal. Not only are they not created equal, a lot of them specialize, so you really need to research and find the proper crowdfunding portal for you.

Ian Formigle, VP of Crowdstreet.com, cautions:

"Online capital formation has taken hold and is gaining strong momentum as a substantial plank of the greater capital markets. If you feel it is a viable solution for your company then there is no better time than the present to begin. When doing so, carefully examine your options; understand the key differences between the platforms (e.g. SPV vs. direct to investor) and select one that you feel confident will serve as a valuable partner to you as you embark in this new arena."

If your project, company or deal gets rejected by one crowdfunding portal, that doesn't necessarily mean that your deal is a bad one and that you can't get funding. It just might mean that particular crowdfunding portal wasn't the right one for you.

Fourth, I mention a lot of companies,

platforms and contributors in this book. Many of the companies are clients are mine, but some are not. A list of contributors are in the back of the book. I strongly encourage you to reach out to some of these resources to help you get your campaign on track – they would love to hear from you! There will also be resources available and discussions galore at our website at TheCrowdfundingMyth.com and on our Facebook page at /TheCrowdfundingMyth – join us and the discussion.

Another myth is that crowdfunding is easy. Money-raising, like anything else worth doing, is not easy. Sorry, but it's not. I know that's not what you wanted to hear, but it's true. It's work. This includes crowdfunding. The myth that has been bandied about is that crowdfunding is the new way to raise money. Actually, crowdfunding has been around forever, just known by other names. It isn't any easier than it was before. Now there's even more competition. There are tons of crowdfunding websites, new ideas and new businesses and they're all looking for the same capital that you are. So you have to set it up correctly. You have to follow the law, go after the right crowdfunding platform, and have your plan put in place.

With all that being said, you can make it easy. You can also make it so it's like shooting fish in a barrel. It can really be that easy. You need to have a system and you need to make people want to come to you.

I recently had a client, we'll call him Joe. Eighteen months ago, he had not raised a dime of private capital. Joe took a class with me and then called me to have a private placement memorandum prepared. A private placement memorandum is the document between yourself and the investors. With it, the investor knows exactly what it is that they're getting into when they invest. You need to have this disclosure. Now you might say, "But I've invested on things like Kickstarter, Indiegogo or PledgeMusic and I've never seen a private placement memorandum. I thought that crowdfunding got rid of private placement memorandum." This is simply not true.

Kickstarter, Indiegogo, and PledgeMusic and similar websites do not have a particular element of securities law in them. We're going to talk about what securities law really means in chapter six and why you need to worry about securities law. We will also talk about when you need a private placement memorandum.

Let's get back to Joe. He deployed the private placement memorandum, and then called me about six months after the ink was dry, saying that he needed another private placement.

I asked him, "Why? What's wrong with the one you have?"

He said, "Nothing. I ran out of room. I sold all of the units and I still have people who want to give me money and I don't want to turn them away."

I said, "OK. But how did you raise that much money so quickly?"

His offering had been written for $2.5 million.

I asked him straight out, "What can I tell others who are struggling to raise funds? What did you do right?"

He said, "Well, it was just as easy as you said it would be. I just needed to hit the ground running, have some confidence, do it right and not be too anxious."

You're no different than Joe. You can have exactly the same success. You need to follow two important steps to be successful.

One, follow this book. Read it over and over again and examine the supplemental material provided on our website. Second, be confident. This might seem really simple, since these are the only two steps. But you're only going to build the confidence you need if you take step number one and follow this book. Confidence may be the biggest issue. We're selling a potential investor on your ideas and business acumen. In many ways, you are selling yourself. If you don't believe in your ideas and acumen, there's no way an investor will believe in you. No one is going to bet on a boxer who lacks confidence that he can win. The same applies here.

One thing real entrepreneurs lose sight of is that their business acumen – it is through their business acumen that they create wealth. An investor's money alone will not create wealth. Why do you think hedge funds managers, mutual fund managers and sports team managers make so much money? It's their acumen and confidence resulting in wealth that delivers the big paycheck. After all, it's not their money they're playing with; it's other people's money. Think of yourself as the big hedge fund manager, mutual fund manager or sports team manager. Money is everywhere. Your business acumen and opportunities are not.

I want you to be confident and continue to realize that cash is a fungible commodity. Despite this, do not forget that cash is indeed king. Cash will make all of your deals just a little easier to close. Cash will make opportunities suddenly appear that were not otherwise unavailable to you. Cash will help you sleep better at night.

The world of investing is a vast and often overwhelming puzzle, sometimes seemingly impossible to complete. This book is a major piece of that puzzle. Better yet, it's the edge pieces. All you have to do is fill in the rest. Now go ahead and breathe a sigh of relief. This book will give you a newfound confidence about your entire business.

So, now that you understand what the crowdfunding myth is, let's get started on raising capital through crowdfunding and review some of the tools that are available to you and your burgeoning enterprise.

## II.  FEAR

*"One of the greatest discoveries a man makes, one of his great surprises, is to find he can do what he was afraid he couldn't do."*
Henry Ford

Fear is a terrible thing. It can really rob us of so many other things in our lives, such as time and opportunities. I want to encourage you not to be fearful when it comes to raising money. Just by reading this book, you are going to have the tools you need to start raising money for your business.

You have to know where to start. But first, I want you to overcome fear. So many times I hear people come to my talks on how to raise private money for their business and they get completely overwhelmed. After getting so overwhelmed they tell me, "It's just too hard. I don't want to do it. I can't. I'm too afraid."

You should know the law. You should understand the marketing principles behind raising private money. That's why you're reading this book. You have to have a fundamental understanding. If you don't have a fundamental understanding, then you are going to fail. But once you have those tools, it's just implementing the tools.

The fear I often hear from people is, "I'm afraid I'm going to go to jail. I'm not going to do it right and I'm going to go to jail." I'm going to tell you right now, just by reading this book; you're not going to go to jail. You have to take some really serious steps in order to go to jail for securities fraud. First, you have to steal people's money. In the ten years that I've been practicing securities law, I've only actually known one person to go to jail for fraud and it wasn't a client.

Karen Hanover was a woman who lived here in Southern California. She claimed to be a commercial real estate investor, an expert, at that. She called me up one day and asked me if I would go to lunch with her to talk about her business. I reluctantly went. At lunch, she asked me if I would be her private money expert at her events throughout the country where she was selling her commercial real estate products and education.

She seemed sincere enough to me, so I agreed to go to her event in Dallas, Texas. I gave a 45-minute talk to a group of hopeful real estate entrepreneurs on how to raise private money, the steps that needed to be taken and what to look out for in the law.

At the end of my talk, Karen came up to the stage and started talking about how amazing I am and how great I was for her business. She made a comment saying that I had helped her raise over $300 million last year. The only problem with her saying this was I had only known Karen for about three months and had not helped her raise even a dime.

Now I know lawyers have a reputation of being liars but this did not sit well with me. After returning home from Dallas, I called another attorney friend of mine and had them run a background check on her. What came up was astounding. Karen Hanover had been going through the state, ripping people off left and right, with everything from cookie sales, to squatting in houses in Orange County, to a variety of other fraudulent activities. I immediately severed ties but unfortunately other people weren't so lucky. Approximately 100 people gave Miss Hanover $30,000 a piece to get them into commercial real estate. Her guarantee was that she would get each individual student into a commercial real estate property within a year. Many months passed and she didn't get anybody into commercial real estate. All of her lies about how she had been in commercial real estate were just that – lies. She had never done one single commercial real estate deal in her life.

Soon the heat was on. People were starting to threaten her. People were starting to lawyer up. So

Karen did the most logical thing. She impersonated an FBI agent. She called several of her students who would be plaintiffs in lawsuits and said, "Hey, you better leave Ms. Hanover alone. This is the FBI." Well, of course people caught on. They actually called the FBI and found out that no one from the FBI had called them. For this she spent 18 months in jail. After she got out of jail for spoofing the FBI, she then was put on trial for fraud and ended up pleading guilty and serving an additional 20 months.

You see, Ms. Hanover made actual efforts to steal people's money. You have to make actual efforts to steal people's money in order to go to jail. So please remove the fear of going to jail for violating securities law.

The point of this story is that you shouldn't be afraid to take action, but don't play ignorant either. You are going to be dealing with other people's money and that, along with the law, must be respected. If you respect people, their money and the law, you won't go to jail.

People also have a fear that their deal is not good enough. Sometimes, that may be true. You really need to know your business and your marketplace. This isn't hard to do. Simple Google searches can give you an idea of what other people are doing and what they're offering in your business and marketplace.

Another fear is that they're not going to be successful with raising private money. Kevin Amolsch is the principal of Pine Financial Group, Inc. Across a variety of offerings and funds, Pine Financial has raised $55 million in private capital to fund private money loans to real estate entrepreneurs.

"I think I have been successful raising money because I have not been afraid to try. I started knowing that I would hear 'no' and just trusted that I would also hear 'yes.' Once I starting bringing money in, it became fairly easy because I became more confident and confidence is all the credibility you need. Raising money is a sales position so I studied sales skills and use a great follow up system. I always did what I said I

<u>would do and I always communicated with my investors</u>. If there was ever a problem I called the investor immediately and discussed it. That went a long way in raising more money." Kevin explains. Interested in assisting other with their goals of becoming entrepreneurs, particularly in the real estate space, Kevin has written *45 Day Investor*, a book available on Amazon. In *45 Day Investor*, Kevin chronicles his entrepreneur journey from purchasing his first house at the age of 21. He gears the book towards anyone looking to buy their first (or next) investment property. In describing his personal path to success, Kevin candidly shares the lessons he's learned along the way so you can sidestep the mistakes and move on to the profits.

In other words, don't let fear drive your business. Lynn Walder is an entrepreneur and crowdfunding investor from Boston, MA. She consistently searches the marketplace for new innovations that are purpose driven. "Ideas are only as good as your ability to execute. Execution requires resourcing, so execution is only as good as your ability to inspire action from those outside of that idea. Don't underestimate the human condition. Everything links back to fear and love (even crowdfunding)."

Now, I'm not telling you to do this alone. I'm not telling you to go out there and just start boldly asking people for money. You need to put a plan in place, or in the words, of Lynn Walder "execute." You need to read this entire book. You need to understand exactly what it is you're asking for and why you're asking for it.

To get over your fear, the first action step I want you to take is to write down your plan. If you write a review of this book on Amazon.com, I will send you a free business plan template. Send a link to your review to info@thecrowdfundingmyth.com (Write the review, whether it is good or bad. I want you to be honest.) I'm not talking about a big, huge, flowery business plan. I'm actually just saying a very simple bullet point plan of the who, what, where, when, how, why and how much. You want to write this down so that you know exactly what your investors are getting into, and you can convey that message to them.

Being prepared will eliminate most of your fears. Robert Gerrard is the Chief Operating Officer of Finaeos, a company that provides a software-based solution for a white-labeled crowdfunding solution, assisting a crowdfunding company with the quest of being "built for equity." He emphasizes the importance of being prepared "A [crowdfunding company] needs to understand what it means to have your company prepared for an equity crowdfunding campaign. They need to understand the financial costs and length of time it takes to prepare for an equity crowdfunding campaign. And lastly, they need to understand that a successful campaign does not happen overnight. There are lots of i's to dot and t's to cross before a campaign can be successful."

So how do you overcome the fear and launch a successful crowdfunding campaign?

1. Develop the right attitude.
2. Have an understanding of the law

(read this book).

3. Write your business plan.

4. Seek out and cultivate relationships with the right people for your team. (You can't crowdfund alone.)

5. Deploy an effective marketing campaign.

6. Care for your investors.

# III.   WRONG ATTITUDE

*"My favorite things in life don't cost any money.
It's really clear that the most precious resource we all
have is time."*
Steve Jobs

Money is fungible. Money is available anywhere. Often I see the wrong attitude with entrepreneurs because they don't understand this concept. Entrepreneurs often lack confidence when they go out to raise money for the first time and give away more than they need to. They may offer things like "personal guarantees." You don't need to offer a personal guarantee. You shouldn't

– it reeks of desperation and no one wants to invest in something that's desperate. Start with the premise that there is money EVERYWHERE and you just need to know how to tap into it. This leads me to my favorite story about one of my heroes, Dr. Phil.

I'm joking! Dr. Phil is not my hero! You can laugh at that. In 2007, I was pregnant with my first child. I had to take a nap at 4 o'clock every afternoon. It was without question. At 4 o'clock, nap time was coming. So I would turn on the TV and Dr. Phil was on. I wasn't a watcher or a fan of Dr. Phil. He just happened to be on at that time every day. One day, Dr. Phil, ever the capitalist, decided that there was a foreclosure crisis coming. He decided to do a special on this impending crisis. He trotted out the most obnoxious couple he could possibly find on earth. This was a couple who just didn't spend responsibly, or at least that is how Dr. Phil made it seem. The family was facing an ever-dwindling bank account, foreclosure, and no prospects of new income after the husband lost his business. Meanwhile, the wife was continuing to spend money on expensive hair extensions, the perfect manicure, and Starbucks every day. They videotaped this woman doing her daily thing: getting her manicure, going to Starbucks, driving in her Cadillac Escalade back to her $800,000 home. They had been able to buy the home with no money down because her husband, as a mortgage broker writing liar loans, had realized a windfall during the real estate boom. This display of overindulgence, luxury and spending and subsequent moaning about it on national television left the audience disdainful of the couple. Despite the disdain, the couple was hurting. They were fighting non-stop because they were fearful of losing their home and their car. It was embarrassing that they might have to move into a smaller home and give up their expensive car.

The couple came on the Dr. Phil show to attempt to get some of their mortgage paid. They believed that Dr. Phil was going to offer them an easy solution. What these people didn't realize is that Dr. Phil was completely exploiting them.

Now, although he was made by Oprah, Dr. Phil isn't Oprah. Oprah loved to quickly solve problems or provide some kind of band aid. She would often buy people cars, pay for things, or tell people to look under their chair for some fabulous prize! But Dr. Phil does not quickly solve problems, give prizes or tell people to "look under their chair" for a new car. Not Dr. Phil. He's there to give you a good tongue-lashing. Dr. Phil has this move he likes to do when he's scolding someone. He doesn't point at you when he's scolding you and he doesn't do the Bill Clinton thumb while he's scolding you. He does somewhere in the middle where it's kind of like a little pointed fist. This poor couple has no idea that they're being made to look like fools on national TV.

Everybody is throwing things at their screen or talking on the internet forums about how annoying this couple is because they bought this house for $800,000 that they couldn't afford. How dare they? How dare they overspend? How dare they buy such an expensive house with no money down? (Side note: I am not siding with this couple's decisions, I am just pointing out that Dr. Phil loves to exploit people…and that's not the point of this story either….stick with me…)

I really felt for these people at one point because you could tell they were so fearful of losing their home and they really believed that Dr. Phil was going to solve all their problems and pay for their mortgage. So Dr. Phil starts scolding them with his little pointy fist. They think this is the moment when their mortgage is going to get paid off and Dr. Phil turns to them and says, "Let me tell you something. All this time you all spend here fighting over this house and money, you are ruining your marriage. You are wasting time. The house is gone!" He straight out tells them that their house will be foreclosed upon. The couple is visibly deflated. But he's not done berating them yet. He continues, "The house is gone. All this time you're spending fighting is wasted while money is fungible." This poor couple didn't want to look any more stupid than they already did, so they leaned back in their chairs and nodded their heads. "Oh, yes, we understand what fungible means." Dr. Phil repeats it to the audience, "Money is fungible." The audience, not wanting to look foolish, just stares at Dr. Phil as if they understand what he is talking about.

You could hear the collective sigh of relief when Dr. Phil threw his arms open and exclaimed, "Fungible means it can be recreated. Money can be recreated. You can get more of it. What you cannot get more of is time. So all this time you're wasting, you can't get back, you can't. So stop fighting over money and work on your marriage."

That's the message I want you to take away from this: You are spending a ton of time on your business, including reading this book. You're also spending a ton of time reading a stupid story about Dr. Phil, but you're loving every minute of it, I know. You're also pending time looking for deals. So when you come across an investor, remember, they are writing checks. All money is the same. There is nothing unique about money. Often, the belief is that "time is money." Change your mindset to "time is precious" because it is –

and your time is no less precious than anybody else's. It's so important to have that attitude when talking to investors. Don't let your investors control the deal, the offer, the rate of return. You are making the offer and you need to maintain control or else investors will walk all over you. After all, they too want the greatest deal. Investors can recognize desperation. They can recognize an entrepreneur or company that lacks confidence. So have the attitude that YOU have the opportunity to provide investors. Investors do not have the opportunity for you. They have money. That's it. That's all they have and there is money everywhere. You've got the opportunity.

Opportunities are abound in smaller companies and private equity. Yale University recognized that there is great opportunity in private equity and as of 2015, had allocated 31% of their assets of their endowment into private equity. In the past 20 years, by investing in alternative investments, they grew their endowment from $3.5 billion to $25 billion.[i]

Think about it; in 2016 alone the stock market

realized $1 trillion in losses.[ii] This has once again, much like 2008, created a class of "stock market refugees." Stock market refugees are those investors who are tired, humbled and confused by the constant volatility and just can't take anymore losses. Investors' retirements and futures are at stake. They are looking for opportunity, not a roller coaster.

If you make the plan, stay legally compliant, put into place the systems and marketing needed, the remains of these stock market refugees could be partly yours. These could be your new investors.

With all of this being said, with your new attitude on raising capital for business and understanding that you hold the keys to the kingdom, never forget that you are a fiduciary to your investors. You must be a good steward of their money. You must follow the law, plan properly, and take the utmost care of your investors' capital. They are trusting you. Betraying that trust will ruin your business and could get you into a lot of legal trouble.

# IV. KICKSTARTER VS. SECURITIES LAWS

*"It takes considerable knowledge just to realize the extent of your own ignorance."*
Thomas Sowell

It is really important to have a basic understanding of the law. If you are selling a security in your crowdfunding campaign, you must comply with securities law.

In 2013, actor Zach Braf appeared on the Howard Stern show to promote his Kickstarter campaign for his film *Wish You Were Here.* Zach was explaining how he raised $2,000,000 in 36 hours and the movie. Howard Stern had never heard of Kickstarter before this. Zach explained the concept to Howard. "Kickstarter is a site where you can pitch an idea, a creative idea to the world. Well, you usually make a video and you have your own webpage and you say here's what I want to do. It could be a movie. It could be a book. It could be music. It could be an innovative – a piece of innovation."

"And you ask people to back you?" asked Howard.

"And you say come back me and I'm going to make this and you're going to be my sponsor. You're going to be a part of this project."

Howard interrupted Zach to ask "Like if I go on Kickstarter and donate 100 bucks to your film, I don't get a piece of the action somewhere down the line, right?"

"You can't, yeah, and this has been one of the things that people have been bemoaning – people who are detractors in this and going crazy about and it's one of the things they're not quite informed about. That's not legal yet. I would have done that in a second. It makes so much more sense." replied Zach.

"Almost like selling stock."

"Yes. And I think that's – people way smarter than me seem to think that's around the corner. You will be able to say, oh, I like Howard. I like the cinematographer. I like that leading lady. I will buy $100 worth of stock in that and then see upside. But that's not currently legal and I don't want to go to jail."

It IS right around the corner, Zach, it's called Regulation CF. But you can still offer securities in the crowdfunding space so long as you fit under another section of the Securities Act of 1933.

See, Kickstarter, Indiegogo, Pledge Music and the like are not selling securities. However, you MIGHT be. Ask yourself these questions:

1. Are you asking for money from investors?
2. Are you using all of the money for the same purpose?
3. Are you (or your company or team) doing all the work to make the money

work?

4. Are you providing a return on
   investment to your investors?

If you answer "yes" to all of these prongs of the test, then selling a security and securities will apply to your crowdfunding campaign.

Kickstarter, Indiegogo, and Pledge Music do not answer "yes" to the fourth prong of the test above as they are not offering profits to investors on any of their campaigns. Think about all the Kickstarter campaigns you may have seen: they fit the other three prongs of the test but they do not offer profits to the potential investors. They're selling a product, a service, a pat on the back or a bumper sticker, something like that. Those are not profits and therefore Kickstarter, PledgeMusic, or Indiegogo do not have to comply with securities laws because they're simply not selling securities.

Zach Braf WANTED to offer securities, but it didn't work for his business model at the time. "The first controversy with the money is when people say, 'All right, cool. But I don't see any upside.' That's bullshit! I agree with you. You're preaching to the choir. I would love to do that and maybe in five years, we will be able to do that. But that's not legal."

Well, it IS legal – you just have to do it legally, Zach. So what if you want to offer a return on investment? What are the steps you need to take to have not just an effective equity or debt campaign, but also a LEGAL one?

Let's start with a little history lesson on securities law. In 1928, the United States saw the massive stock market crash that lead the country into the worst economic depression it had ever seen. In 1932, President Franklin D. Roosevelt was elected into office. As part of his presidency and in response to the Great Depression, President Roosevelt introduced the New Deal: a series of programs enacted between 1933 and 1938. They included both laws passed by Congress as well as Presidential executive orders. The programs were in response to the Great Depression, and focused on what historians refer to as the "3 Rs," Relief, Recovery, and Reform:

Relief for the unemployed and poor; recovery of the economy to normal levels; reform of the financial system to prevent a repeat depression.

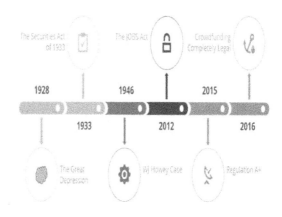

As part of the third "R" – reform – the Securities Act of 1933 was enacted to prevent a repeated stock market crash. It is still good law today.

Despite the Securities Act of 1933, there was still confusion about what a security actually was. The test I gave you above was declared in the Supreme Court case of Securities and Exchange Commission v. W. J. Howey Co., 328 U.S. 293 (1946). The Howey case held that the offer of a land sales and service contract was an "investment contract" within the meaning of the Securities Act of 1933, 15 U.S.C. § 77b, and that the use of the mails and interstate commerce in the offer and sale of these securities was a violation of §5 of the Act,15 U.S.C. § 77e. This is why it is so important that you understand at least a little of the law before you actually learn the "how-to's" on raising money.

The defendants, W. J. Howey Co. and Howey-in-the-Hills Service, Inc., were corporations organized under the laws of the state of Florida. W. J. Howey owned large tracts of citrus groves in Florida. Howey kept half of the groves for its own use, and sold real estate contracts for the other half to finance its future developments. Howey would sell the land for a uniform price per acre (or per fraction of an acre for smaller parcels), and convey to the purchaser a warranty deed upon payment in full of the purchase price. The purchaser of the land could then lease it back to the service company Howey-in-the-Hills via a service contract, who would tend to the land, and harvest, pool, and market the produce. The service contract gave Howey-in-the-Hills "full and complete" possession of the land specified in the contract, leaving no right of entry or any right to the produce harvested. Purchasers of the land had the option of making other service arrangements, but W. J. Howey, in its advertising materials, stressed the superiority of Howey-in-the-Hills' service.

Howey marketed the land through a resort hotel it owned in the area, promising significant profits in the sales pitch it provided to those parties who expressed interest in the groves. Most of the purchasers of the land were not Florida residents, nor were they farmers. They were business and professional people who were inexperienced in agriculture and lacked the skill or equipment to tend to the land by themselves. Howey had not filed any registration statement with the Securities and Exchange Commission. The SEC filed suit to obtain an injunction forbidding the defendants from using the mails and instrumentalities of interstate commerce in the offer and sale of unregistered and nonexempt securities in violation of 5(a) of the Securities Act of 1933.

The Court found that the above transaction constituted an "investment contract" within the meaning of §2(1) of the Securities Act of 1933.

From this, the Court formulated a test determining whether an instrument qualifies as an "investment contract" (now referred to as the Howey test):

1. Investment of money due to
2. An expectation of profits arising from
3. A common enterprise
4. Which depends solely on the efforts of a promoter or third party

Therefore, when searching for investors, it is pretty clear, that even if you place the name of an individual on the DEED of a property, the INVESTOR is still relying on you (a third party) to gain a profit. Therefore, you are selling a security.

You can call it whatever you want: joint venture, mortgage interest (which, by definition, is the sale of a "real estate security"), equity partner, or promissory note, the fact is that it is STILL A SECURITY. Therefore, when looking for INVESTORS or taking money from most any party for your real estate venture, you are selling a security.

Still not convinced? Well, how about this: Under Section 2(a)(1) of the Securities Act of 1933, "unless the context otherwise requires," the term "security" includes any note, stock, treasury stock, security future, bond, debenture, evidence of indebtedness, certificate of interest or participation in any profit-sharing agreement, collateral-trust certificate, preorganization certificate or subscription, transferable share, investment contract, voting-trust certificate, certificate of deposit for a security, fractional undivided interest in oil, gas, or other mineral rights, any put, call, straddle, option, or privilege on any security, certificate of deposit, or group or index of securities (including any interest therein or based on the value thereof), or any put, call, straddle, option, or privilege entered into a national securities exchange relating to foreign currency, or, in general, any interest or instrument commonly known as a "security", or any certificate of interest or participation in, temporary or interim certificate for, receipt for, guarantee of, or warrantor right to subscribe to or purchase, any of the foregoing.

WARNING: CALLING THE SALE OF YOUR SECURITIES A JOINT VENTURE WILL NOT WORK. Unless you have ONE investor that is in the business of investing in real estate, calling your deal a joint venture will not get you out of complying with securities laws.

Now let's apply this to the earlier days of crowdfunding, when the concept of raising money from the crowd seemed like a relatively novel idea. The difference between the crowdfunding platforms then and now was in what they actually offered. We've already established that Kickstarter and Indiegogo are not selling securities but Prosper, Lending Club, and ProFounder all were.

All of them, in one form or the other, fit all four prongs of the test. ProFounder, Lending Club, and Prosper were all in charge of collecting the profits and distributing them back to the investor.

Those crowdfunding platforms that were selling securities were attempting to use a lesser used and somewhat risky rule under the Securities Act of 1933. They were using an exemption known as "Regulation D, Rule 504" which allowed them to raise small amounts of capital from the general public without registering the security. But the Securities Exchange Commission didn't like it. I discuss this at length in the chapter on Title III: Regulation CF and Rule 147.

What have crowdfunding companies been doing? To date, those that are selling securities have been relying on Title II of the JOBS Act which carved out a new section of Rule 506 called Rule 506(c). We go into this in depth in Chapter on Title II and Rule 506(c). What does this all look like? Here's a little chart to refer back to in case you are more of a visual person. This will also help you understand the rest of book.

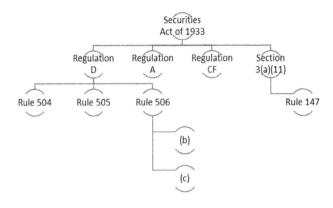

# V.   THE JOBS ACT

In January of 2012, the JOBS (Jumpstart Our Business Startups) Act was introduced to Congress as some kind of saving grace for small business. Prior to its introduction, many crowdfunding portals were operating under the exemption provided by Rule 504 of Regulation D. Rule 504, allowed, in part, for Crowdfunding companies to raise up to $1 million in a 12 month period, without regard to suitability requirements and general solicitation rules.

The JOBS Act impacts four areas of securities laws: creation of Crowdfunding portals, expansion of Regulation D to include a new section under 506, expansion of Regulation A, and advantages for "emerging growth companies" that are publicly registered. The chart below illustrates the advantages for each title.

| TITLE I: **Creates new "Emerging Growth Company" class with exemptions for those Crowdfunding companies that fall into that class.** | Creates an 'on-ramp' for IPOs from Emerging Growth Companies, with confidential SEC staff review of draft IPO registration statements, scaled disclosure requirements, no restrictions on test-the-waters communications with qualified institutional buyers (QIBs) and institutional accredited investors before and after filing a registration statement, and fewer restrictions on research (including research by participating underwriters) around the time of an offering. |
|---|---|
| TITLE II: **Carve out of a new exemption under the newly formed 506(c)** | Allows for general solicitation of investors under a newly created 506(c) so long as the Issuer only sells to 3rd |

| | party verified accredited investors.[1] |
|---|---|
| **TITLE III:**<br>**Establish a Small**<br>**Offering Exemption**<br>**for Crowdfunding** | Allows small Crowdfunding companies to raise no more than $1,000,000 through an SEC approved crowdfunding portal. |
| **TITLE IV:**<br>**Expansion of**<br>**Regulation A to**<br>**include a 2nd Tier**<br>**(also referred to as**<br>**Reg A+)** | Allows the Issuer to raise up to $50 million in a 12 month period, with few, if any investor suitability requirements. |

## *TITLE I:*

### *Smaller funds and issuers going public*

For many, it doesn't make sense for a small fund or Issuer to go public if they lack operating history and financial resources for the audits, legal work, and ongoing compliance. However, many smaller Issuers have found that going public opens the doors to a larger capital market.

---

1 An "accredited investor" is defined under Rule 501 of Regulation D. Generally speaking, it refers to an individual who earns $200,000 per year, a married couple that earns $300,000 per year, or an individual or married couple that has a net worth of $1,000,000 exclusive of their primary residence.

Poverty Dignified is a small public company based in North Carolina. Poverty Dignified established itself as a business incubation company developing micro-franchise business concepts designed to affect the individual, community and local economy in rural and peri-urban areas across the globe. Poverty Dignified focuses its efforts in the continent of Africa. Their strategy in going public was to reach a broader audience of purpose-driven investors. They hope to list their stock on the OTCQX at some point in the near future so that their shareholders may enjoy the ability to trade in a public marketplace.

Poverty Dignified is also hoping that their status as a public company will expose them to a variety of hedge funds, investment bankers, and other "funders" in the stock market space as well as bigger trusts and charitable organizations that invest in public equity.

Title I's newly created "Emerging Growth Company" class allows those public companies that earned less than $1 billion in gross annual revenues to more easily and confidentially file for an initial public offering without fear of retribution from the SEC for not fully complying with certain SEC rules or sections of Dodd-Frank. Title I is pushing forth the hope of the SEC and the creators of the JOBS Act to encourage smaller issuers to go public.

Poverty Dignified ™

is an incubation company cultivating indigenous ideas into micro-franchise businesses, strategically designed to turn poverty into prosperity.

## TITLE II:
### The creation of 506(c)

On September 23, 2013, the Rule 506(c) of Regulation D became effective allowing small companies and private investment funds to use "general solicitation" to reach accredited investors, which means they may advertise or publicize an offering on the internet, radio, television, billboards, and other mediums. Those offerings offered under Rule 505 and Rule 506(b) will still continue to be prohibited from using general solicitation to reach investors.

### TITLE III:
### For those looking for small amounts of capital

Title III of the JOBS act allows issuers to raise up to $1 million within any 12-month period from investors without triggering the registration requirements of the Securities Act of 1933, as long as the transactions are made through an SEC-approved broker or funding portal. It's great if an issuer just needs small amounts of money from smaller investors. No investor may invest more than 10% of their net worth or a maximum of $10,000. This leaves a small issuer with the need to convince at least 100 investors to invest in their deal just to raise a mere $1,000,000. This is great for the first time real estate investor or private money lender, but not helpful for expanding to bigger projects and deals.

### Title IV:
### Regulation A – kind of like a mini-IPO

A common complaint heard around the capital- raising world is about the limitations that Regulation D places on advertising and solicitation. Issuers often feel that they have used up their own personal rolodexes of investors and really need to be able to look elsewhere. Feeling trapped, Crowdfunding companies are not able to effectively grow their business because they can't obtain sufficient capital in their current circle of investors and they don't know how to find new investors without advertising.

For some crowdfunding companies, Regulation A can solve this problem. Before the JOBS Act, Regulation A allowed an Issuer to raise up to $5 million in a 12 month period through the means of general solicitation. There is little to no qualification required of investors, who need not be accredited under Regulation A. Unlike a public "registered" offering, however, Regulation A filings do not have ongoing reporting requirements nor do they require financial audits.

The JOBS Act carves out a new section of Regulation A, referred to often as "Tier 2" or "Reg A+", that will allow to the Issuer to raise up to $50 million in a 12 month period, with few, if any investor suitability requirements.

# VI.   THE OLD LAW IS STILL THE GOOD LAW

*"Do not let spacious plans for a new world divert your energies from saving what is left of the old."*
Winston Churchill

In order to raise money quickly and without SEC approval, many crowdfunding companies will use a private offering. Private offerings are regulated under Regulation D of the Securities Act of 1933. Regulation D is actually an exemption that allows a company to raise money and sell securities without registration with the SEC. The most popular choices are an offering under Rule 506(b) (the old rule) or 506(c) (the new rule under Title II).

Rules to follow in doing a private offering

under Rule 504, 505, or 506(b):

- No general solicitation or advertising of the security is allowed. This means you cannot use the US Mail system or any other means of interstate commerce. You cannot use the media: newspapers, magazines, radio, and television specifically stating the sale of the security. You may not conduct seminars where a specific offering is promoted. You also may NOT CROWDFUND and likewise, you cannot make an offer on your website.

If you do want to put information on your website, like your offering documents, under these rules, take these steps:

1. Must be approached by potential investor and provide all pertinent information.
2. Investor must be a qualified purchaser and the information provided must be confirmed.

3.  Potential investor may be given a specific password that is unique to them and expires.
4.  With this password, qualified purchasers may view the offering materials.

- You must have a substantive pre-existing relationship with the investor.

### What does a "substantive pre-existing relationship" mean?

A "substantive" relationship is one that allows the offeror (you) to determine that "each of the proposed offerees currently has such knowledge and experience in financial and business matters that he or she is capable of evaluating the merits and risks of the prospective investment."

Although a substantive relationship is usually established by a past business relationship, it may also be established by "questionnaires that provide the offeror with sufficient information to evaluate the prospective offerees' sophistication and financial circumstances;" however, the relationship is not pre-existing if the questionnaire and offer are distributed at the same time.

A pre-existing substantive relationship must be present even where the offeror has reason to believe that the offerees are persons of financial means and experienced in business affairs. *In the Matter of Kenman Corporation, 1985 SEC LEXIS 1717 at *9.*

Under the Securities Act of 1933, any offer to sell securities must either be registered with the SEC or meet an exemption. Regulation D (or Reg D) contains three rules providing exemptions from the registration requirements, allowing some companies to offer and sell their securities without having to register the securities with the SEC.

However, not all exemptions are "self-executing" and you still must inform the state of the use of such use of exemption. These laws vary from state to state. Furthermore, under Regulation D, particularly Rule 505 and 506, companies are restricted on the number of unaccredited investors and may be limited to accredited investors.

An accredited investor is basically a smart person with lots of money. However it's a little more complex than that. An "accredited investor" is defined under Rule 501 of the 1933 Act and has the following requirements for one to be deemed accredited:

- Any person and their spouse with a combined net worth of $1,000,000 (exclusive of their primary residence) OR

- Any person with an individual income of $200,000 in the two most recent years with a reasonable expectation of reaching the same income level in the current year OR

- Any person and their spouse with a combined income of $300,000 in each of the two most recent years with a reasonable expectation of reaching the same income level in the current year.

Rule 501 also has accreditation requirements for entities such as other companies, trusts, or other organizations:

- Any trust with total assets in excess of $5,000,000, not formed for the specific purpose of acquiring the securities offered, whose purchase is directed by a sophisticated person.
- Any entity where the equity owners are accredited investors.

### *Which Rule Do I Fall Under?*

### **Rule 506**

Rule 506 is considered a "safe harbor" security and is the most lenient in terms of disclosure, but has the most restriction on the type and number of investors. Because it is a "safe harbor" and it is shielded from many of the securities laws of the states, a 506(b) previously was the most popular choice. For those companies not using crowdfunding to raise money, it remains the most popular choice. A Rule 506 offering may be made to unlimited accredited investors, but only up to 35 "sophisticated investors." Therefore, those without proper investing experience or the ability to understand the investment in particular, may not invest.

*"Sophisticated investors are investors that must have sufficient knowledge and experience in financial and business matters to make them capable of evaluating the merits and risks of the prospective investment"*

In re: Dambro 51 SEC 513, 517 (1993)

Under Rule 506, companies may raise unlimited funds. Companies may decide what information to give to accredited investors, so long as it does not violate the antifraud prohibitions of the federal securities laws. But companies must give sophisticated investors disclosure documents that are generally the same as those used in registered offerings. If a company provides information to accredited investors, it must make this information available to non-accredited investors as well.

*Filing Requirements with the SEC when using the Regulation D exemptions:*

While companies using a Regulation D exemption must file what's known as a "Form D" after they first sell their securities. This is not a registration statement and no continuing reporting is required. The Form D is an application that includes the names and addresses of the company's management and agents, which exemption it is relying upon, what kind of securities are being sold, and how much is being sold.

Form D's may be filed electronically through the EDGAR system to the SEC. (See the Chapter on Regulation A for more information.) Many states also allow electronic filing of the FORM D along with the payment of a filing fee.

### Rule 505

In the past, I have done Rule 505 offerings for my clients because they offer a certain level of flexibility when it came to allowing unaccredited investors to invest. However, many states are sticklers on when the FORM D is filed under Rule 505 and some state even require filing the offering documents as well. This leaves the money raising entrepreneur open to scrutiny by the state securities boards. That's not something you really want.

Rule 505 allows the raising of up to $5,000,000 among an unlimited number of accredited investors and up to 35 unaccredited investors. In addition, specific, semi-specific, and blind pools are allowed under this exemption. There is, however, a restriction on resales. Investment must be made for investment purposes only. Rule 505 also has some rules regarding financial statements:

- Financial statements need to be certified by an independent public accountant – however, they need not be audited.

Furthermore, most new companies will not have any financial statements, therefore, financial statements will simply not be provided.

- If a company other than a limited partnership cannot obtain audited financial statements without unreasonable effort or expense, only the company's balance sheet (to be dated within 120 days of the start of the offering) must be audited; and

- Limited partnerships unable to obtain required financial statements without unreasonable effort or expense may furnish audited financial statements prepared under the federal income tax laws. (Unclear if this also applies to limited liability companies)

Again, these depend on the availability of financial statements. A new company will not have financial statements as there will have been limited activity.

## Rule 504

Rule 504 provides an exemption for the offer and sale of up to $1,000,000 of securities in a 12-month period. Even if you make a private sale in a state where there is no specific disclosure delivery requirement, you should take care to provide sufficient information to investors to avoid violating the antifraud provisions of the securities laws. While companies using the Rule 504 exemption do not have to register their securities and usually do not have to file reports with the SEC, they must file what is known as a "Form D" after they first sell their securities.

- The total amount raised may not exceed $1,000,000 within a 12 month period

- Sold to unlimited number of unaccredited investors

- General Solicitation is ALLOWED if the state where the security is offered allows it and the investors must be accredited. You must use a state exemption that allows you to advertise and only advertise to accredited investors.

- The offering cannot be a blind pool.
- States generally have their own disclosure requirements.

You can also use this exemption for a public offering of your securities and investors will receive freely tradable securities under the following circumstances:

- The offering is registered exclusively in one or more states that require registration.
- The offering is registered and sold in a state that requires registration and disclosure delivery and also sold in a state without those requirements. You must deliver the disclosure documents mandated by the state in which you registered to all purchasers.
- The offering is sold exclusively according to state law exemptions that permit general solicitation and advertising, so long as you sell only to "accredited

investors."

- Active steps are taken to ensure you are not selling securities to non-accredited investors.

- You sell "restricted" securities, meaning that they may not sell the securities without registration or an applicable exemption.

I am personally not a fan of Rule 504 in its current state. The SEC claims they intend to amend Rule 504 to be increased to $5,000,000. However, many states don't even allow Rule 504 offerings. Every single time I have done such an offering for a client, I have provided them with strict warnings: do not take investors from the following states (like Michigan or New Hampshire.) Without fail, every single time, the client doesn't listen and ends up with an investor in a forbidden state. It becomes too much of a hassle. We will see what the new rules bring.

# VII.  TITLE II: THE NEW 506(C)

*"With the new day comes new strength and new thoughts."*
Eleanor Roosevelt

Let's talk about the rule many crowdfunding companies would be most likely to use from the JOBS Act for a crowdfunding campaign: Title II. Title II carved out a new rule under Rule 506 subdividing Rule 506 into two areas: 506(b) (previously discussed) and 506(c) (the new rule). Under Rule 506(b), the investor has to tell the truth about their status as an accredited investor, however, under 506(c), that liability shifts to the crowdfunding company, and in some case, the crowdfunding portal. To date, many crowdfunding portals have been relying on Rule 506(c) to conduct crowdfunding campaigns.

Fundrise, a real estate crowdfunding platform, was able to offer its accredited investors an opportunity to invest in World Trade Center 3 under Rule 506(c).

Under 506(c), a crowdfunding company can still raise an unlimited amount of money just like under Rule 506(b) – in other words, a crowdfunding company can raise as much money as they want. However, unlike Rule 506(b), there is no room for any investor that is not accredited. This includes sophisticated investors. All of the investors under Rule 506(c) must be accredited investors, meaning investors that have an income

of $200,000 a year as an individual, $300,000 a
year as a married couple or have a net worth of a
million dollars exclusive of their primary
residence.

It is on the shoulders of the crowdfunding
company to verify that an investor is truly
accredited. The new rules have multiple ways that
accreditation may be verified such as a letter from
a CPA, registered investment advisor (RIA), or an
attorney; review of certain financial documents;
third party verification.

This is all new as of September 2013. A
crowdfunding company still must provide proper
disclosures like a private placement memorandum.
A Form D must be filed with the SEC and the
states – just the same as under 506(b). Why would
a crowdfunding company want to do this if there
exists this burden of verifying that all the investors
are accredited? Because now the crowdfunding
company can advertise the opportunity like on a
crowdfunding platform.

This changes the game. This new rule allows

crowdfunding among accredited investors. You could throw up a Facebook advertisement saying, "Offering eight percent preferred return. Call us today." It's just that when your phone rings, you must verify that the potential investor that is about to write you a check is actually accredited.

One platform that takes advantage of the general solicitation allowed under Rule 506(c) is Crowdstreet. CrowdStreet is a software and services company disrupting the commercial real estate industry by enabling innovative real estate operators and developers to efficiently engage in online capital formation, communicate with investors, distribute investment documents and centralize ongoing investor relations. CrowdStreet technology solutions provide real estate sponsors a scalable platform for managing a large investor-base. CrowdStreet Marketplace allows sponsors access to a national audience of accredited investors. CrowdStreet Sponsor Direct enables enterprise-level sponsors to use the same technology powering the CrowdStreet Marketplace to present offerings to their own investors, under their own brand. Both CrowdStreet solutions democratize access to commercial real estate investment opportunities by connecting accredited investors, family offices and institutions with real estate sponsors for no-fee co-investing, and modern digital portfolio management. Take a look at the front page of Crowdstreet.com's website.

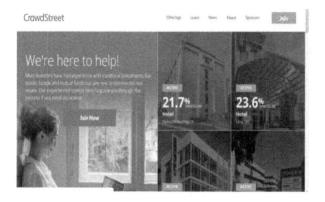

Here's a list of the steps a crowdfunding company must take when conducting an offering under Rule 506(c):

1. **Offerings may only be sold to accredited investors.** 506(c) offerings must be sold to accredited investors only. This, for many

crowdfunding companies, may exclude family members or previous investors who do not have the income or net worth requirements of accredited investors under Rule 501.

2.  **Those accredited investors must be verified as accredited.** This shifts the burden to the issuer from the investor of accreditation status. An issuer can verify the investor in a number of ways:

    - Income-Based Verification – Copies of any IRS document that shows income (W-2, K-1, 1099, 1040, etc.) for the two most recent years, along with written verification that investor will reach accredited limits in the current year.
    - Net Worth-Based Verification – A copy, within the past three months, of the following: Bank statements, brokerage statements and other statements of securities holdings, certificates of deposit, tax assessments and appraisal reports issued by independent third

parties; a credit report from at least one of the nationwide consumer reporting agencies is required; and written statement that all liabilities necessary to make a determination of net worth have been disclosed.

- <u>Third-Party Verification</u> – written confirmation from a registered broker-dealer, an SEC-registered investment adviser, a licensed attorney, or a certified public accountant that such person or entity has taken reasonable steps to verify that the purchaser is an accredited investor within the prior three months and has determined that such purchaser is an accredited investor.  Other persons could potentially serve as third party verifiers, subject to additional rules.

- <u>Roll-Over Accredited</u> – Those people who were treated as accredited investors under a prior 506 offering by the same issuer are deemed to be accredited investors in future 506(c) offerings, provided that such investor certifies that he is an accredited investor.

3.  **Voluntary submittal of advertising materials.** The SEC has also created a portal on its site for uploading of advertising materials by those relying on Rule 506(c). Uploading is entirely voluntary and is kept confidential. The uploading portal may be found here: https://www.sec.gov/forms/rule506c

Anecdotal evidence suggests that this new rule may not truly benefit the smaller Issuer, but rather the big hedge fund or REIT looking to spread its message faster and easier to accredited investors. These are the crowdfunding companies that can readily place an ad in the New York Times or Wall Street Journal without fear of cost or consequence. With many larger funds and firms that have brand recognition, the competition to draw in accredited investors is fierce for a smaller issuer. Coupled with the hassle of accredited verification, many crowdfunding companies have elected to instead stick with a Rule 505 or Rule

506(b) offering and take a more personal approach to attracting investors.

### *Soliciting Investors on your Own Website Under 506(c)*

When it comes to verifying investors for your own crowdfunding campaign on your own website, I want you to hire a third party verification system. Why? Because then you shift the liability from you onto the third party verification system. To my current clients, I recommend two companies for this type of service: VerifyInvestor.com and FundAmerica.com.

Scott Purcell is the CEO of FundAmerica.com, the crowdfunding industry's premier provider of escrow, transaction engine technology, anti-money laundering services, transfer agent services and other back-office systems. In advising those looking to set up their own crowdfunding portal or website to advertise an investment opportunity, Scott is very clear, "respect the fact that you are issuing 'securities' and that you have a lot of new legal 'stuff' to deal with. Hire your attorney and your marketing people accordingly." This includes having your investors verified properly by using a system like FundAmerica.com.

# VIII.    THE REAL
# CROWDFUNDING RULE:
# TITLE III

*"Crowdfunding as an idea itself isn't new - bands have
been doing it since the dawn of time."*
Amanda Palmer


The whole reason the JOBS Act was created in
the first place was because of Title III – which is
now being called "Regulation CF." Title III was
the reason the JOBS Act came about. There were
multiple websites out there like Lending Club,
Prosper.com, and ProFounder, which all offered
that new thing called "crowdfunding" in one form
or the other. But quite frankly, crowdfunding has
been around forever and ever and ever.

Take a look at Fundable's "History of
Crowdfunding" and you can see that

crowdfunding has really been around since the 1700's when Jonathan Swift founded the Irish Loan Fund which lent money to low-income families in rural Ireland. Thereafter (much like the modern crowdfunding websites today) there was a proliferation of over 300 programs throughout Ireland.

Fast forward to 2005 and the micro-lending website Kiva.com was launched, providing individuals with the opportunity to lend money to entrepreneurs in poverty stricken areas throughout the world. Shortly after, the investing marketplace saw sites like Lending Club, Prosper, and ProFounder spending millions of dollars to market their unique brands of crowdfunding. How are they doing it? Prior to the introduction of the JOBS Act, many crowdfunding portals were operating under the exemption provided by Rule 504 of Regulation D. Rule 504 allowed, in part, for Issuers to raise up to $1 million in a 12 month period without regard to suitability requirements and general solicitation rules. Crowdfunding portals such as Profunder.com operated this way for years without doing any kind of registration with the Securities Exchange Commission or the state securities boards beyond filing a Form D.

ProFunder.com, specifically, sold project dependent notes and equity interests to investors. Each investment opportunity in total was less than $1 million. Anyone could invest and the opportunities were all over the internet (general solicitation). Profunder's claim, much like Lending Club and Prosper.com, was that they could do these types of offerings under Rule 504.

However, the Securities Exchange Commission didn't like it too much. Actually, they didn't like it at all. All of this was too big, too fast, and too much. In the wake of the rampant fraud of Bernie Madoff and other securities scandals, the SEC believed these sites might be a breeding ground for fraud. These platforms could present an opportunity that would take advantage of investors. This was when the cease-and-desist orders went out. They went out to Lending Club. They went out to Prosper. They went out to

ProFounder.

In January of 2012, the JOBS Act was introduced to Congress as some kind of saving grace for small business. Unfortunately, the regulators felt that ProFounder, and others like them were not applying the law appropriately, forcing ProFounder to shut its doors in February 2012. It wasn't until April 2012 that the President signed the JOBS Act into law. At that time it was too late for ProFounder, but it opened the doors for new crowdfunding portals. Lending Club and Prosper.co took different approaches, choosing instead file as publicly traded companies. They remain that way to this day.

All of these crowdfunding portals got very agitated. They couldn't believe that their business was being shut down by the evil SEC. They put forth a proposition to congress, out of which came the JOBS Act. We are here now discussing Title III, the "crowdfunding regulation" or "regulation crowdfunding."

So all of that work, worry, and pain felt by all

of these crowdfunding portals and regulation crowdfunding is still not legal. We won't see it be legal until about May 16, 2016. What will happen once it is legal? Here are some of the highlights:

- Companies will be able to raise up to $1,000,000 in a 12-month period.
- The crowdfunding company can have as many investors as it wants.
- Investors do not have to be accredited or sophisticated, meaning *practically anyone can invest.*
- An individual investor will be able to invest up to $100,000 across all crowdfunding platforms in any given 12-month period. However, investors' individual limits may be lower depending on their annual income or net worth.
- Investors with an annual income or net worth of less than $100,000 are limited to the greater of $2,000 or 5% of their annual income or net worth (whichever is less).
- Investors who have an annual income or

net worth of more than $100,000 are permitted to invest up to 10% of either their annual income or their net worth (whichever is less).

- Crowdfunding companies that wish to operate under Regulation CF will only be able to do so under a regulated platform – meaning that crowdfunding companies will not be able to rely on Regulation CF to raise capital on their own websites (unless, of course, they are a regulated platform).

- Crowdfunding companies may only use one crowdfunding portal at a time.

- Crowdfunding companies that are raising more than $500,000 are going to need to get an audit every year and the only place they may advertise for their crowdfunding is through a crowdfunding campaign in one portal.

- Under the final rules, for crowdfunding companies raising up to $100,000, only an internal financial statement review must be conducted and provided to the crowdfunding platform and investors. Those raising between $100,000 and $500,000 must have CPA-reviewed financial statements. Generally, companies raising between $500,000 and $1 million must have third-party audited financial statements in order to be in compliance with the final rules. However, companies that are first-time crowdfunders raising more than $500,000 are exempt from the requirement to provide audited financial statements and, instead, can submit CPA-reviewed financials to investors and the intermediary assisting with the raise.

At the end of the day, when regulation crowdfunding is finally legalized, it will be interesting to see who even uses the JOBS Act. Why? Because all of the sales are going to have to go through the portal. The only advertising that can happen has to go through the portal. It's going to be fee-based. This is very unfortunate for the little guy in a lot of ways. So many companies come to me barely able to pay for the audit, the securities attorney etc., and now they are going to have to pay all of these people to raise a measly $2,000 from each individual investor. That seems like a lot of upfront cost for little in return.

### *Rules for the Funding Portals*

The crowdfunding portals wishing to host crowdfunding companies under Regulation CF are also going to have some rules to follow. These crowdfunding portals must be registered as a "funding portal" with the SEC and become a member of the Financial Industry Regulatory Authority (FINRA), which is the official national securities association. The funding portals will also be responsible for investor disclosure. You can be sure that this expense (the cost of a securities attorney and auditor) will be passed ultimately to the crowdfunding company, even though the funding portals themselves face an independent requirement to take measures to reduce fraud and ensure companies provide investors with educational materials that present a clear explanation of the process for investing, the types of securities offered, any limitations on resale of those securities, and total investment limits. Funding portals will also be subject to a series of rules that govern the provision of access to their crowdfunding portals, intermediary conduct, and compensation to their promoters.

Additionally, platforms must provide a method that is seamless for communication so that questions and concerns about the securities being offered are addressed. Portals will also need to comply with confirmation, completion and cancellation of securities offerings requirements. This seems like a lot of risk for a funding portal to take on smaller deals like those that will be offered under Regulation CF.

***So if Regulation Crowdfunding isn't even legal, what's every equity or debt platform using? Are they operating illegally?***

No. CrowdStreet, Patch of Land, StartEngine, Crowdfunder, CollectiveSun, and Fundrise do not use Regulation CF. They are using some other exemption or offering. Many of them are using are using Rule 506(c), which means that the opportunities on most of these sites are only available to accredited investors. Some are using Regulation A so that a greater pool of people is able to invest. One crowdfunding site mentioned above, CollectiveSun, isn't using Regulation A or Rule 506(c). Instead, they are using the little used exemption under the Rule 147 of Section 3(a)(11) of the Securities Act of 1933, otherwise known as the "intrastate offering exemption." The intrastate offering exemption generally allows a company to raise funds in its home state without having to register under the Securities Act of 1933.

### *Intrastate Offerings under Rule 147*

Under the intrastate offering exemption a crowdfunding company may raise money without fear of retribution from the federal government so long as:

- The company must be incorporated in the state in which it is offering the securities.
- The company must carry out a

significant portion of its business in that state, which is defined as at least 80% of its operations.

- The company must only sell the securities to individuals residing in the state of incorporation.

Even though a crowdfunding company could conceivably sell securities out from underneath the thumb of the federal government under this rule, they must still follow the rules in the state in which the company intends to "crowdfund." For example, the state of California has a process called "Registration by Permit"2 where a crowdfunding company can register the securities with the state. Upon approval by the Department of Business Oversight in California, a crowdfunding company can use the internet and other means of advertising to attract in-state investors. Even better, the SEC is considering lifting some of the restrictions of Rule 147 to make an offering like this even easier. As of May

---

2 Registration by Permit in the state of California is under Section 25113 of the Corporations Code of California.

16, 2016, the SEC proposes to eliminate the current restriction on offers under Rule 147, while continuing to require that sales be made only to residents of the issuer's state or territory. The proposed amendments also would redefine what it means to be an "intrastate offering." This would ease some of the issuer eligibility requirements in the current rule, making the rule available to a greater number of businesses seeking intrastate financing.

CollectiveSun, a platform based in San Diego, CA, focuses on impact investing that uses the power of the community to help nonprofits raise the funds to achieve financial and environmental sustainability with solar power. Non-profits typically face challenges when it comes to financing solar power for their real estate. CollectiveSun provides a solution for these non-profits by providing a place for the non-profit to fundraise for power.

Lee Barken, Chief Community Officer, faced his own challenge when it came to securities regulations. With Regulation CF not even close to legal in 2012, Lee had to figure something out to keep the power on, so to speak. "We opted to explore a California Permit. This limited us to California projects and California investors, but for a time, we could work with this." After all, there is plenty of sunshine and people in California. For CollectiveSun, the intrastate offering in California made perfect sense.

CollectiveSun obtained its first permit in 2014 and renewed the permit in 2015, allowing California investors to invest in the solar power of non-profit organizations in California. CollectiveSun can be found at collectivesun.com

Intrastate offerings are absolutely fantastic for those crowdfunding companies that are located in a large state and have no reason to leave that state. Although we were the law firm that obtained the permit for CollectiveSun, truthfully, they were the only non-real estate permit we ever obtained. It is my experience that real estate related companies that are operating in their own home states are the ones that benefit the most from the intrastate exemption and the California Permit process.

In reviewing the future for CollectiveSun, although they have had incredible success within the California marketplace, they are consistently bombarded with requests from non-profits from around the country. Unfortunately, until Regulation CF is complete or CollectiveSun finds another alternative to Rule 147, they will be staying in California.

For many crowdfunding companies, Regulation CF does not make much sense as it only allows up to $1,000,000 and the investors can't invest a lot of capital. But for those non-profit entities that wish to have their solar projects crowdfunded on CollectiveSun, Regulation CF will make a lot of sense. CollectiveSun has a minimum investment requirement of $25. Further, most of the projects on CollectiveSun are less than a $100,000 raise. Therefore, many of the pains of Regulation CF (such as investor prequalification) will not apply to the projects on CollectiveSun, if CollectiveSun so chooses to offer deals and opportunities under Regulation CF.

Lynn Walder, entrepreneur and crowdfunding

investor, is not counting out Regulation CF. She and WeFunder.com (a site on which she invests) are excited about the prospect of smaller investors with small amounts of capital getting into the game. "I personally am committed to leveling the field where every individual has the ability to invest, no matter what their net worth." WeFunder and Lynn concentrate on purpose driven campaigns. It is most likely those (just like CollectiveSun) will be the companies that most benefit from Regulation CF.

If your business model will benefit from small investments of less than $2,000 from everybody, than Regulation CF might work for you. Regardless of what you decide for your crowdfunding campaign, you still have to make proper disclosures. So all of the stuff we're going to be talking about with disclosures doesn't go away, even with Regulation CF.

Certain disclosures are still required of businesses under Regulation CF. Companies will be required to provide and periodically update detailed information to their crowdfunding portal and investors as well as file a new Form C with the SEC. Companies that use Form C will be required to file annual reports with the SEC. In addition to details about the company and its securities, information provided to portals, investors, and the SEC will have to include specific financial information.

### *Regulation CF and Rule 147 working in tandem*

Jennifer Gatewood, PMP, is the principal of Peer Elevate, a crowdfunding platform based in Mississippi. Peer Elevate Funding is currently conducting intrastate offerings in Mississippi, registering in Florida, then moving to other states. In addition, they are finalizing preparations for Title III offerings. They have already started receiving inquiries from potential clients for Title III. When the updated 504 regulations are approved, they believe they will offer those as well.

"I see Title III working in tandem with the intrastate state rules. Title III gives the alumni and transplants a chance to give back to their home state. The offering document can be done in such a way that both state and federal rules can be ran concurrently." notes Jennifer.

Jennifer wants her issuers to be well rounded and educated, so she heads up two organizations in the "Peer" empire:

PeerElevate.com is education-oriented, providing an online academy for professionals, businesses and investors. They are currently developing and seeking course content to create interactive eBooks, recorded classes, quizzes, interactive presentations, social media integration and search engine optimization. The education platform allows industry experts to publish their content, provide free or paid courses, and market their services and resources.

PeerElevateFunding.com is a custom built, proprietary registered, regulation crowdfunding platform. It is developed for crowdfunding using intrastate rules, Title III and future national regulations.

However, Jennifer is selective in who gets to showcase themselves: "While I am the principal member, I utilize a screened network of trusted professionals and select contractors to support the platform and issuers." Peer Elevate has quite the laundry list of requirements for a potential crowdfunding company to be listed.

*Not to worry - there are choices.*

Maybe with all of these rules for a small amount of capital, Regulation CF is not going to work for your crowdfunding campaign. However you have many other types of offerings that you can do:

1. A non-securities based offering such as those offerings on Kickstarter, Indiegogo, etc.
2. An offering to accredited investors only under Regulation 506(c) (Title II of the JOBS ACT.)
3. A mini-IPO offering to all potential investors under Regulation A.
4. An offering to just those investors in your

state under Rule 147 of Section 3(a)(11). *WARNING: this type of offering will ONLY work if you are able to STAY within the state in which you are operating.* It is my experience that this type of offering only works in larger states (both in size and population) such as California, Texas, Colorado, and Florida and usually can only work for those types of companies that can remain local (like in-state real estate related ventures.)

# IX. REGULATION A+ - BIG DEALS FOR SMALL INVESTORS

*"I welcome and seek your ideas, but do not bring me small ideas; bring me big ideas to match our future."*
Arnold Schwarzenegger

## Regulation A, Pre-JOBS Act: An Exercise in Futility

Prior to the JOBS Act, Regulation A filings were stuck in the basement of the Securities Exchange Commission. It rarely saw the light of day and when it did, the SEC attorneys, having never really seen them before, didn't know what to do with them. This caused incredible delays and hardships for companies attempting to raise money with Regulation A.

Regulation A filings pre-JOBS were onerous and not worth the time or expense. Pre-JOBS Regulation A only allowed companies to raise up to $5,000,000 in a twelve-month period and this was only after a very lengthy process of being approved by the SEC that involved paper filings, unlike the online filing that public companies enjoy through the SEC's EDGAR system. EDGAR stands for Electronic Data Gathering, Analysis, and Retrieval. All public companies (and now, Regulation A companies) are on this system and are searchable. To search for a company, simply go to sec.gov and click "company filings" in the top right hand corner. You can then enter in any public company name, including Regulation A filings, and all the filings for that particular company will be available for review so long as filings have not been made confidentially. Companies, particularly smaller ones, are allowed to file confidentially so that their information does not appear on the EDGAR system until their offering has been fully vetted and approved by the Securities Exchange Commission.

Previously, companies attempting a Regulation A were forced to mail in seven copies of their filing every time a change was required in their offering documents. This proved to be extremely cumbersome, as most filings exceeded 100 pages. Moreover, the company would have to anxiously await a response from the SEC without confirmation as to whether their filing reached the proper person or was actually being processed by the SEC. On more than one occasion, the SEC lost my 700 page filing. It was devastating and depressing. I would have to call the client and humbly explain that we had no idea where their filing went. Yes, I sent it FEDEX. Yes, I required a signature. This didn't stop the SEC from misplacing all 700 pages. (Did I mention this happened more than once?) Sometimes, weeks later, the filing would end up back in my office in some mystery box without explanation.

Since the JOBS Act, the Regulation A filing process has become so much easier. By being able to file on the EDGAR system, companies are able to see their uploaded filing in real time, if they don't file it confidentially. If a company does choose to file confidentially, then the filer will be able to receive a confirmation of receipt from the EDGAR system.

Regulation A filings were difficult and not just because of the SEC. What made it worse were securities attorneys. Most of them didn't even want to touch a Regulation A filing with a ten-foot pole, making it impossible for a company to even attempt money raising under Regulation A, as they didn't even have a qualified attorney to file the paperwork for them.

In 2008, our firm started doing Regulation A offerings. I am not even sure why I agreed to do them, as they were painstaking to both me and the client. True story: a Regulation A filing is the only reason I have ever literally cried over the phone to the SEC. That was *ahem* embarrassing, to say the least. I got over it. I am not sure the SEC attorney did. Oh well.

Back in the day, Regulation A offerings to an attorney were like garlic to a vampire. I only met one other attorney, other than myself, who had even attempted one. According to a search of the EDGAR system, between 2008 and 2013, I had done 40% of the Regulation A filings for real estate. This is not saying much considering I think I only did 3 of them. In 2011, my firm had the only approved Regulation A filing.

## *Post-JOBS: The Exciting Era of Regulation A+*

On June 19, 2015, the SEC adopted Title IV of the JOBS Act, facilitating easier access to private capital formation for small companies. Title IV is colloquially and legally called "Regulation A+." Regulation A+ updates and expands on the former Regulation A exemption and carves out two new sets of rules, Tier 1 and Tier 2, with annual limits of $20,000,000 and $50,000,000, respectively, that small securities companies can legally use to advertise and raise capital from private investors.

In September 2013, the SEC authorized advertising to accredited investors under a new

Regulation D, Rule 506(c) exemption pursuant to Title II of the JOBS Act. However, because it is estimated that only 10% of all investors in the US are accredited, this shuts out a lot of quality investors from investing in smaller, private companies.

Regulation A+ seeks to solve that problem by allowing advertising of securities offerings to the general public with a streamlined pre-approval process. Under Tier II, anyone can invest up to 10% of their net worth or 10% of their gross annual income (whichever is greater). This opens up a new audience for companies who can't access enough accredited investors to fund their deals, and who already know a lot of unaccredited (and deserving) investors who would like to invest with them. After all, an individual with an income of $199,999 and a net worth of $999,999 would not be an accredited investor. Having offerings that are only available to accredited investors shuts out a large part of the population that clearly has the means to invest.

I live in area called the Temecula Valley

located in southern California. Temecula is situated about 60 miles north of San Diego, 45 minutes east of Orange County, and 90 miles southeast of Los Angeles. Temecula is a great city with farms, families, and wineries. Many of the residents of Temecula commute to San Diego or Orange County for work. Of those that are employed, 59% are employed in a white collar job. The average household income in Temecula is approximately $92,000. It truly is a lovely place – but that's not my point. My point is the residents of Temecula are people who have good jobs they will not be quitting any time soon. Many of them may not have the income or net worth of many of those that live over the hills in Orange County, but don't count these potential investors out; they have good jobs, incomes, and a desire to invest in crowdfunding. Regulation A+ crowdfunding opportunities will serve not just your purposes as a crowdfunding company, but the investment purposes of potential investors like those residents of Temecula, CA.

But Temecula is not an anomaly. They are not

the only vestige that holds your potential investors. Good, quality, deserving investors (35% of the total population to be exact) have a net worth that exceeds $100,000. [iii] The average American has an income of $51,000 per year.[iv] Regulation A is offering this AMAZING opportunity to crowdfunding companies and to investors alike. For the first time ever, smaller investors will have access to opportunities that were only previously available to accredited investors. Crowdfunding companies, generally smaller companies that don't have access to venture capital, angel investors, or even accredited investors, will now be able to tap into this investor market unlike ever before. It's a win for everyone including the SEC, because unlike traditional private offerings, the SEC will have some level of oversight on all of these investment opportunities due to the newly implemented review process and reporting process that I describe in the rest of this chapter.

### *Tier 1 (changes to Regulation A)*

Under Tier 1, a company may now raise up to

$20,000,000 as opposed to the old $5,000,000 limitation.

Tier 1 does not have any audit requirements. This is great for those companies looking to save on audit and accounting costs, however this does not provide the investor audited financials of the company. It is important for potential investors to be aware of the company that doesn't bother with a financial audit and ask themselves, "Why? Was the audit too cumbersome? Is the company perhaps hiding something? Or was the expense not worth it?" Audits can get quite expensive, but often give investors the peace of mind of transparency when a company is audited. Because a Tier 1 filing does not require an audit or have much in the way of ongoing reporting requirements, a Tier 1 company still must "blue sky" their offering. This means in order to sell their securities, a Tier 1 company must subject themselves to the scrutiny of the individual states where they intend to sell. Additionally, Tier 1 companies must pay the corresponding review fees for such states, which could potentially exceed the cost of an audit. This makes Tier 2 a more appealing option for those who wish to raise money from investors in multiple states.

Investors should be aware that if a company does decide to go the route of Tier 1, it might simply be because they are only conducting business in a couple of states and not because of any nefarious reason. After all, a Tier 1 filing is not just reviewed by the Securities Exchange Commission, but also by the state regulators where the company is selling the securities.

Kevin Amolsch of Pine Financial Group, Inc. conducted multiple offerings under Regulation D in his home state of Colorado and in Minnesota. In the effort of full disclosure to investors, the state securities boards in both Minnesota and Colorado, and the SEC, he elected to conduct an offering under Tier I. "It makes the most sense because we can reach more investors and be completely transparent with all interested parties." His current offering is being reviewed by the SEC.

## Tier 2 (the new Regulation A+)

Tier 2 of Regulation A will allow companies who meet $50,000,000 in a 12-month period. Tier 2, like Tier 1, will allow for uploading of filings to the EDGAR system and general solicitation. Tier 2 companies will be required to perform an audit prior to approval and for a minimum of three years following approval. The Tier 2 company must also hire a transfer agent and meet certain ongoing reporting requirements similar to a public "smaller reporting company". Tier 2 companies would be required to file a Form 1-k within 120 days after the company's fiscal year end, semi-annual reports on a Form 1-SA within 90 days after the end of the first six months of the company's fiscal year end, current reports on Form 1-U, and exit reports on Form 1-Z.

Despite the additional requirements, Tier 2 pre-empts the state pre-approval requirements under Tier 1. Therefore, the Tier 2 company would not have to "get permission" from every state in which they wish to sell.

### The Value in Testing the Waters

Both Tier 1 and Tier 2 companies will be able to enjoy the benefits of testing the waters. In most states and at the federal level, companies will be able to file advertising materials that a company plans to utilize to gauge interest prior to approval of their offering. This is helpful for companies to figure out what to offer investors, what would be of interest to investors, and to build a prospective investor list.

While testing the waters, companies may solicit potential investors prior to even drafting an application for approval with the SEC or the states, but they cannot collect any money from anyone until the SEC approves such an application. During this phase, companies may collect indications of interest in their company or opportunity for later contact and sale once their Regulation A offering is approved.

### Changing Crowdfunding

Crowdfunding is a weird term. It has been

used to describe many things, but "Regulation Crowdfunding" in its purest definition allows a company to raise up to only $1,000,000 from the crowd on a regulated "funding portal." Investors would not be allowed to invest more than 10% of their net worth or $10,000, whichever is less. Most "crowdfunding portals" are operating under Rule 506(c) or some other exemption or rule in order to reach the crowd for companies and projects.

StartEngine.com, a crowdfunding portal out of Los Angeles, focuses its platform on Regulation A offerings. It is banking on the increased potential number of investors that the Regulation A rules have to offer. Unlike portals that only support 506(c) offerings where only accredited investors are allowed to invest, Regulation A offerings will allow the entire crowd to invest. This is a difference of nine million potential investors to the entire estimated 300 million-person population of the United States.

To prove the power of the crowd, StartEngine supported the launch of Elio Motors and their

Regulation A offering. After testing the waters for a month, Elio Motors had an astounding $25 million in commitments from investors through the StartEngine portal before their Regulation A offering was even approved by the SEC.

### *Why Regulation A+ will provide a wealth of opportunities for all involved*

According to Bain & Company's Global Private Equity Report 2015, private equity holdings, on average, realized double digit gains in 2014 and was expected to continue the trend in 2015. In May 2015, Pension and Investments reported that U.S. private equity performance has largely mirrored that of public equities over the five-year period. For longer periods of time, however, the private equity index exhibits significantly higher returns on an annualized basis, providing a nice return for investors.

Further, and as stated earlier, most of the opportunities in private equity investments are restricted to the 3% of the population deemed accredited investors. It is as if a private club only available to the wealthy exists, leaving the common man investor out of the opportunities that often provide the greatest return. Since 2009, 95% of the income gains have gone to the top 1%. Regulation A may work towards creating a shift where the investment income generated from smaller companies goes, with the hopes of shifting it to a greater percentage of the population.

Despite the attractive returns, there are multiple issues when it comes to investing in private equity opportunities. First, there is very little liquidity (if any at all) for private securities. This means that the investor must wait to almost provide the opportunity to or "allow" an investor to sell before an investor can dispose of their interest in private equity. There is no "private equity" stock market and most limited partnership or limited liability company interests are further restricted by the governing documents of the company such as a limited partnership agreement or operating agreement.

Regulation A will also solve some liquidity issues for some crowdfunding companies that choose to take advantage of it on behalf of their investors. A stock corporation issuer might look to getting their stock listed on a smaller exchange such as the OTCQB or OTCQX. These over-the-counter exchanges are NASDAQ trading platforms where smaller companies can apply to trade their stock. From an investor perspective, purchasing Regulation A stocks that are traded on the OTCQB and OTCQX will be no different than purchasing stock that is traded on the NYSE, NASDAQ or some other exchange. In most cases, an investor will be able to login to any online brokerage account (like E-Trade, Scottrade, etc.) and purchase Regulation A company stock in the secondary market. In addition, shareholders will be able to use the same brokerage accounts to sell their stock. Please note that not all Regulation A offerings will be available on these exchanges as not all Regulation A filings will qualify for the exchanges and not all crowdfunding companies will want to have trading stock. Therefore, investors should read the offering documents fully and ask any questions regarding liquidity prior to investing. Each Regulation A offering may have its own plan of liquidity, redemption, or exit strategy.

Cherif Medawar owned over $50 million in various real estate assets located in California and the US territory of Puerto Rico. He was training his students in his training company to invest and build wealth in the same manner. His personal portfolio in the mid 2000's included unique historic mix use commercial properties that he was able to revitalize in Old San Juan, Puerto Rico to acquire some of the biggest retail brand names such as Burberry, Puma, Coach, Tommy Hilfiger, Sunglass Hut, Guess, and Perfumania etc.

In the late 2000's Cherif realized that the best way for his students to grow was to offer them a way to invest with him. He quickly became a fund manager and launched his operation to expand in California using private money along with his own capital under Regulation D, Rule 506(b) using "Education based marketing" to attract investors.

Cherif also had the foresight to have his fund focus on investments in California where he purchases and renovates multimillion-dollar single family homes and resells them for tens of millions to high end buyers from around the globe (www.migsif.com).

Although his fund grew and as of early 2015 he had over $100 Million Dollars of assets under management between his personal portfolio and his syndicated fund, he came to me asking for help. Many of his students from his education company, www.cmrei.com, were getting frustrated because they were not accredited and could not join him in his real estate endeavors.

Once we spoke about the incredible opportunities he could offer his students and investors under the new Regulation A+, including the potential to list it on the over-the-counter marketplace, he wanted to be one of the first fund managers to launch this structure in the US.

After the finalization of the rules in June 2015, Cherif set out to start a new fund entitled the "United Group Fund" (www.UGFinc.com). According to the prospectus available on

EDGAR, United Group Fund intends to sell preferred shares that will eventually list on the OTC marketplace. "I wanted to allow my investors to have not only reliable dividends, but also good liquidity. I thought attempting to get the shares listed on an over-the-counter public marketplace, might be attractive to investors worldwide," notes Cherif.

The process was direct and simple. After a couple of brief phone conversations, Cherif and I were able to creatively structure his fund in a way that could potentially help him grow tenfold, with his students and investors. He will continue to expand and our plan to go public (over-the-counter) will only turbo his methods to raise capital and deploy it in valuable real estate assets.

This is the dramatic difference I was able to offer him with the Reg. A+ that we could not offer under Reg. D 506(b) or (c) in the past.

What is exciting for me as an experienced attorney, is the fact that not only was I able to help him achieve his vision, but I was also able to help his students partner up with him and/or invest directly with him instead of trying to risk it all on their own without help or guidance.

His previous personal success and depth of real estate investing experience have been attractive to his students and other potential investors for many years and they flocked to his rare live trainings and events in California. But only the accredited ones were able to join him. Now the game has changed completely thanks to Regulation A+ and the ability to list it on the Over the Counter Marketplace.

### Investment Disclosures Reviewed by the Securities Exchange Commission

Besides lack of access and liquidity issues, a major problem with private equity or debt offerings is the lack of information available to investors prior to investing. Companies seeking capital from private investors are required by law to disclose all the material facts so that an investor may make an informed investment decision. Despite the "rules" surrounding this disclosure, no regulatory agency reviews the offering documents, such as a private placement memorandum, prior to dissemination to potential investors. A Regulation A offering must be approved, and thus reviewed, by the Securities Exchange Commission before any investment may be made by investors. In the case of Tier 1 offerings, the Regulation A offering is reviewed not only by the Securities Exchange Commission, but also by the individual state securities regulation authorities in every state in which the securities are sold. Those Regulation A offerings that are sold by a broker dealer may go through even further scrutiny by multiple attorneys and by FINRA (Financial Industry Regulatory Authority), the self-governing body that provides licenses to brokers and agents of securities sales.

### *The Buyer must still always be aware*

Despite all the review a Regulation A may go through, a buyer must still always beware prior to investing. Most companies taking advantage of Regulation A are smaller companies. Many are startups that have absolutely no assets, little cash, no operations, and an unproven business model. Those companies using Regulation A to grow their business are most likely in need of capital for one reason or another; they are not filing a Regulation A to make the founders or current shareholders wealthy (like some public companies such as Facebook and Tesla have been known to do in recent history). Larger companies, blue chips even, that "go public" will not use Regulation A and instead will continue to participate in a traditional Initial Public Offering (IPO) to get their stock to the marketplace.

Even if the companies using Regulation A were larger, well-established companies, this does not shield them from potential fraud. History has shown us that even the largest, most well established companies can be rife with fraud, mismanagement, and incorrect projections. Twenty years ago, we saw large energy firm Enron commit such massive fraud that shareholders (most of whom were employees) lost everything and there was a major movement to change the law regarding the responsibility of publicly traded companies and their independent auditors. More recently, we saw major blue chip, mostly banks that were "too big to fail," realize massive losses, in large part at the expense of the shareholders.

In the private sector, the world saw former Chairman of NASDAQ, Bernie Madoff defraud major pension funds, charities, and celebrities. Some brilliant financial minds invested in Mr. Madoff's private funds and did not predict or know of the fraudulent behavior that was resulting in the disappearance of investors' funds.

Besides fraudulent or criminal behavior, an investment could become a loser for a multitude of other reasons such as unpredictable fluctuations in a particular marketplace, downturns in the economy, the death or leaving of a key employee that leaves the business in bad position, a failed business model, or a bad business decision. Regulation A companies would not be exempt from any of these risks or potential circumstances.

There will still be an abundance of

opportunities in the Regulation A offering marketplace for investors. Investors should look to take the following steps in evaluating a Regulation A offering opportunity prior to investing:

1. Read the entire offering document. Many investors, due to time constraints or just an unwillingness to do so, neglect to read the carefully (or maybe not so carefully) prepared offering documents. Companies have prepared these offering documents so that investors are fully informed of the risks and the plan of the business. It's important that an investor read the documents so they understand exactly what the expectations of the company are.

2. Understand what is being offered and what exactly the company is doing. Investors should just avoid offerings that don't make sense to them. The offering itself might make a lot of sense. It might be a great opportunity that will yield great returns. However, if the individual investor does

not understand the business model, the plan, or the offering, then they should not invest. Investors who follow this advice will be following the footsteps of Warren Buffet who famously refused to invest in technology stocks or companies in the early 2000's because he did not understand the market.

3.  Verify that the company is doing what they say they are going to do. Regulation A offering companies are required to provide certain reports to their investors. Investors should make sure that the company making the offering has kept up with those reports. A potential investor should read these reports along with the offering documents to determine if the company is sticking with timelines previously promised and determine if the company is reaching its goals.

These are just a few suggestions on steps to take prior to investing in any offering, including Regulation A offerings. Investors should have their own checklist of items they are looking for in an offer, in a company, or in the management of the company. Individual investors will have different risk profiles or return requirements leading to different opportunities for different investors. Whatever the case may be, it is an exciting time to be an investor or a startup company and to see the vast array of opportunities that new Regulation A will bring to the marketplace.

# X.   POSITIONING & MARKETING

*"Money coming in says I've made the right marketing decisions."*
Adam Osborne

Most investors don't invest because you overtly ask them to. Instead, most investors invest because they like the positioning of the company, they have heard of them, and/or they believe in what they are doing. This is why branding and positioning your company may be even more important and effective than just out and out ask*ing for an investor to invest their money.

Scott Whaley started the Real Estate Investors Funding Association at the dawn of the JOBS Act and now hosts the annual REIFACON for real estate crowdfunding. "A crowdfunding campaign is successful not because of great pitches or great technology or even great implementation. I believe it is successful because the crowd that it serves buys into it due to the services it provides, the timing and the simplicity of the idea and the obvious advantages it gains for those who support it." says Scott. "Crowdfunding campaigns fail because those crowdfunders look at the crowd as just another group to sell stuff to for the people who are the promoters. They then try and sell them on investments or ideas that are marginal and really not what the crowd, or at least the crowd they reach, wants."

Think of all the great companies that you wish you got in with on the bottom floor: Google, Apple, Blackstone Realty, your local house flipper that's done really well for him or herself. What did they do? They most likely didn't ask for money overtly. Instead, they showed potential investors how great they were. They used marketing of their company and their brand and their spectacular products to get people excited and interested. I see this happen now in green tech – potential investors get excited about an idea or the potential of an idea or they are attracted to the brilliance of the officers of the company. Think about Elon Musk. He is the founder, CEO and CTO of SpaceX, co-founder, CEO and product architect of Tesla Motors, chairman of SolarCity, co-chairman of OpenAI, co-founder of Zip2, and co-founder of PayPal. Two of these companies are two of the biggest green tech companies today: Solar City and Tesla Motors. Both companies give the investor something to care about.

"Many entrepreneurs believe that if you build a campaign profile on Kickstarter or Crowdfunder, the crowd will just come. This is not 'Field of Dreams' - if you build it, they will come. It's imperative to have a well thought out integrated campaign prior to launch," emphasizes Melinda Moore, the president of Moore Media Ventures. She is a social entrepreneur, a seasoned digital marketer and a frequent speaker at leading technology conferences. Previously, Melinda was Chief Marketing Officer for Crowdfunder.com.

During her tenure, she successfully launched a campaign for iFunding, a real estate crowdfunding platform (see, even crowdfunding platforms need to crowdfund). In a short 48 hours, iFunding, with Melinda's help, was able to raise $1 million on Crowdfunder.com.

Melinda's advice to others looking to achieve the same results is clear: "Make sure your product or idea has a crystal clear value proposition and that people will care and be passionate about it. Does it pass the 'who cares' test?"

See the Facebook advertisement for Moikit below. Although they are conducting a campaign on IndieGoGo, they clearly see the need and value of advertising on Facebook for additional customers and support.

This is the same thing you need to do for your company. Get investors to be ATTRACTED to you with proper publicity. Asking for money or announcing great returns has two problems: it may be illegal and it never ever works. Think about it; how many times have YOU received an email that says "get 18% return on investment." Did you actually invest? No, because there is no excitement, no attraction, all risk (despite the email saying "no risk" to be sure).

Jay Goth heads up InSoCal Connect, a non-profit organization that helps entrepreneurs achieve success by connecting them to the mentors, resources and capital they need. He has seen many companies try to grab at funding and very few be successful. When asked what it takes to be successful, he stated simply,

"Marketing.
Marketing.
Marketing.
Value of Product.
Marketing."

Jay points to the success of the Pebble Watch campaign. The value proposition to the end user was simple: a watch that did everything an iWatch did but way less expensive. Simple, right? Pebble Watch backed this "value of product" up with a strong marketing campaign including multiple press releases and strategically placed advertisements.

## 9. Pebble

Pebble had long been making smart watches before Apple Watch was released. It had one of the most successful Kickstarter campaigns of all time. For their first product they were able to raise over $10 million in about 30 days on Kickstarter. Within their first year it had sold over 400,000 watches!

They are definitely not a one hit wonder – **Pebble raised a record-shattering $20 million on Kickstarter** for its second generation watch.

*Courtesy of "10 Insanely Successful Startups." http://tech.co/successful-hardware-startups-2016-02 by John Teel*

Pebble Watch continues to take care of their customer/investors by providing updates and excitement. This leads to brand loyalty.

*Pebble press release in 02/2016:*

Create the excitement. Tell the investor why you are exciting. It will not be your "fabulous returns" – they can get that anywhere. Be mysterious. Be the cool kid that has a little bit of intrigue that people want to know more about. Don't be desperate. No one is ever attracted to desperation.

Things to think about:

- Do you have a web presence? If so, is it slick and attractive? Does it speak to a particular audience?
- Do you have a logo? Is it professional looking? Does it look like you spent time and/or money on it?
- Do you have relatable, memorable company name?
- Are you in the "community" – whether it be online or in your actual community?
- Do people know who you are?

If you answered "no" to any of these questions, get to it! What are you waiting for?

Justin Belleme of JB Media Group assists mostly "purpose driven" campaigns with their marketing efforts. He talks about two of his successful campaigns below:

"One of the most successful campaigns was the Appalach Custom Fitted Sweaters campaign, which raised $55,000 through Kickstarter. We also assisted with the Outrider Horizon Adaptive Electric Bike campaign on Kickstart which raised $126,000. For both campaigns we provided campaign strategy and coaching for the client marketing team and direct support for social media, public relations, and online advertising. Both campaigns took a tremendous amount of effort for both our team and the client team as well.

"For Appalach, they started with a heavy push to family and friends to get the funds flowing. We then reached out to many related media outlets because their campaign was innovative from a sustainable fashion and fashion technology perspective. Small press release hits turned into larger ones and the pre-orders started coming in.

Despite the coolness factor of the first 3d Printed Wool Sweater, we did not hit any major viral successes or any huge press release hits directly for the campaign. The client got several great press release hits that were not about the campaign but which came in as a result of the campaign efforts. The pre-orders came in steadily but even with steady orders the campaign still required a few fairly large family and friends contributions in order to be fully funded.

"For Outrider, we started with family and friends again. The campaign had a great video which really helped. The campaign also had around seven promotional partners which were non-profits or recreational organizations that were offered a reduced price electric bike in exchange for supporting the marketing. As with Appalatch we also did massive press release outreach to nearly 1,000 outlets. Again, the small pickups led to larger press release wins. The campaign also worked with several influencers or celebrities who are known in the target market and their content about the campaign really helped us reach the right audience. This was a big ticket purchase item so the first orders took a while to come in. Some of the first customers required a test ride on the prototype or further proof of concept. After about two weeks the campaign was about 25% funded but there had not been any pre-orders for the full product. Around half of the way through, we had our first order and then one order per day for three days in a row – this resulted in about 50% funded.

"The following week the momentum continued with one order per day for 3 days in a row and then we had a huge day with three orders totaling over $25,000 – this got us fully funded with one week left. The final week saw around four more orders bringing the total to $126,000. The success of the campaign led to several more very high profile press release pickups."

I asked Justin, "What made these campaigns so successful?" He not only gave the answer, but provided a simple list for you to follow for your own campaign:

"Both campaigns had a clear target audience, strong early support from family and friends, a strong press release and social media strategy and intense effort from the founders of these companies and our team. All of these projects had at least four team members working hard for several months before and during the full run of the campaign."

### *Marketing Strategy*

According to Justin, for a crowdfunding campaign to be a success a company should "schedule at least two to three months for strategy and planning. Build your audiences on social and email before the campaign. Happy existing customers and close family and friends are your best allies in a campaign but you must have an effective and efficient way to get them involved and you must have a backup plan if your existing audience does not get you the momentum that you need to fuel the campaign."

Melinda Moore of Moore Media Ventures wasn't short of advice either. (And you should take it! She is an expert in crowdfunding and digital strategy. She has helped launch over 100+ crowdfunding campaigns including ones for Yao Ming, Laird Hamilton, Quincy Jones, and Kevin Harrington.) She generously compiled this easy to follow list on steps to take to insure a successful launch:

1. Have a great story and strong messaging. iFunding had a clear value proposition for the company. Real estate is tangible and people understand the real estate investing space.

2. Have a well thought out, integrated marketing campaign with PR, video, social outreach and customer relationship management tools and software. The CEO of iFunding generated lots for press with a press release and television appearance on CNBC's Power Pitch.

3. Have a strong management team that understands crowdfunding. The management team at iFunding clearly understood the crowdfunding space.

4.   Have traction in the first couple of days of your campaign. This means having your friends and family lined up to invest, deploying your marketing ahead of time and working closely with your portal to insure success.

# XI.  PUTTING IT ALL TOGETHER

*"By failing to prepare, you are preparing to fail."*
Benjamin Franklin

### *All the Steps: a quick snap shot*

Before you start going to raise money, let's go through the steps you are going to have to take on a macro level. Ian Formigle shares what is critical for a successful campaign from CrowdStreet's perspective:

1.  Professional Materials – a professionally articulated investor presentation with a well-rounded corresponding document set (e.g. pro forma, sales comparables, rent

comparables, third party reports, investor documents and market data) is a key first step in demonstrating professionalism and expertise on the part of the sponsor.

2. Compelling Business Plan – In conjunction with high quality materials, sponsors that can present a logical and compelling business plan outperform. Investors are attracted to groups that demonstrate a proven ability to attract customers.

3. Allotting Sufficient Time – While campaigns timelines can be accelerated, allotting 30 – 45 days of platform time exposure enables sponsors to let the process run its natural course. Certain investors may be skittish and back away from an investment if they feel hurried to invest.

4. Sponsor Interview – CrowdStreet typically posts a sponsor video interview within two weeks of an offering launch, which consists of a voice recording of the key principals discussing its company, the

asset and its business plan against a backdrop of slides. In an online world, a video interview of a sponsor conveying its enthusiasm for the subject acquisition is a viable substitute for a sponsor-investor conversation.

5. Sponsor Willingness to Engage with Investors – While not always necessary, given CrowdStreet's "Direct to Investor" model, it is important for sponsors to be open and available for direct investor engagement.

6. Transparency – The world of online capital formation is predicated on transparency from all participants (sponsor, investor and platform). Sponsors should be prepared to openly participate in sharing information.

7. Competitive Returns – With each and every offering it posts, CrowdStreet drives transparency across all sponsors, including investor terms and targeted returns. If sponsors wish to enter the CrowdStreet Marketplace, success often translates to

being willing to "meet the market."

8. Strong Reporting – Communication is the number one factor in building investor trust, which highly correlates to funding success. Therefore, CrowdStreet seeks sponsors who demonstrate the capability to deliver strong investor reporting on a quarterly basis.

Although these eight points above are CrowdStreet specific, they really do apply to any campaign, with the exception of the real estate specific items. There are many things for which you need to be aware, prepared, and ready. First and foremost, as we saw from previous chapters, you need to organize yourself internally before you can go out and present your company externally. In between all of this, you need to actually put your offering together.

"Lack of preparation and understanding of what an investor needs to know in order to make an evaluation, determine risk, and determine whether they want to make that investment are the real reasons a campaign is a failure. A lot of people think that if you post something, everyone will come. That couldn't be further from the truth. You have to work just as hard to get through the fundraising round. How the company is presented needs to be very well thought out." warns Amy Wan of Patch of Land. This includes the offering documents.

Once you have your offering together, it is imperative to QUALIFY your investors prior to providing them with your Offering documents. How will you need to qualify them? Well, that will depend on how you are raising money.

Let's take a review:

| Rule 506(b) Offering | Up to 35 sophisticated investors and unlimited accredited investors. NO GENERAL SOLICITATION. Not best for crowdfunding |
|---|---|
| Rule 506(c) Offering | Accredited Investors Only |
| Regulation A Offering | Anyone can invest but only up to 10% of income or net worth pursuant to Rule 251(d) |
| Regulation CF | No more than 5% of net worth or $2,000 per investor |

*Things to think about: What you need to disclose to potential investors.*

Your investors are relying on you to give them all the information that they need to invest. Furthermore, it's the law to disclose any "material information that would influence an investor's decision to invest."

Here are some items that the law believes are material:

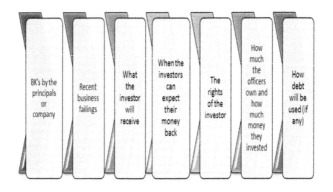

BK's by the principals or company | Recent business failings | What the investor will receive | When the investors can expect their money back | The rights of the investor | How much the officers own and how much money they invested | How debt will be used (if any)

## *The Anatomy of a Private Placement Memorandum*

The Private Placement Memorandum ("PPM") is the document a crowdfunding company might use to present their investment opportunity to a potential investor – generally speaking an offering under Rule 506(c). (A similar document, prepared by an attorney and presented to the SEC is used for Regulation A offerings.) Upon agreeing to invest after attesting to reading and understanding the PPM and its exhibits, the individual will receive a subscription agreement to fill out. The subscription agreement is the contract that states the following by the investor:

1. That they understand the PPM and have read it fully;
2. That they understand what they are purchasing;
3. That they agree to purchase and tender purchase money with the subscription agreement;
4. How they would like to receive payment of distributions/profits/interest and where such payment shall be delivered.

Prior to getting to the point of filling out the subscription agreement, an investor must read the private placement memorandum which will have the following potential categories:

**Cover Page**
- States the offering price, Type of offering, Allowed investors, Minimum purchase, Summary

**Securities Legends**
- Required text by the securities boards and SEC; Only include the legends applicable - the legends that are for the states in which you are offering the security

**Suitability Standards**
- Accredited Investors, Unaccredited, and/or Sophisticated

**Summary**
- What the investors will get, what to expect, what the company is all about

**Risk Factors**
- What the risks are related to investing in the securities, related to the company, the mangement, the industry

**Use of Proceeds**
- How the investors' money will be spent, what percentages will be spent where, whether or not commissions/due diligence fees will be paid.

**Dilution**
- How the security might be effected by internal and external circumstances.

**Company**
- Description of the company, its business, its plan, and its management.

**Management**
- Who the officers and directors are. What their experience is. What their compensation may be.

**Tax and Legal**
- What kind of tax treatment investors may expect; any litigation or other controversies effecting the company.

**Exit Strategy**
- How investors may expect to be paid back and how they may redeem their interests.

**Exhibits**
- Any exhibits pertaining other pertinent information or disclosures.

This chart is merely an outline. I implore you to consult a legal professional prior to deploying any private placement memorandum. As an attorney, I am going to strongly recommend that you use the services of a competent attorney – one that understands securities laws – to put your private placement together. This chart is merely provided to you as guide.

With that being said, I also want to discourage you from buying a template online. These are generally junk and you will get what you pay for. A trained professional will know what should and should not be in your private placement memorandum.

The same goes for Regulation A offerings. An attorney is going to know how to get you through the process with fewer headaches.

If you are still unsure of where to start, use the chart on the following page as a quick guide to some of the decisions you need to make.

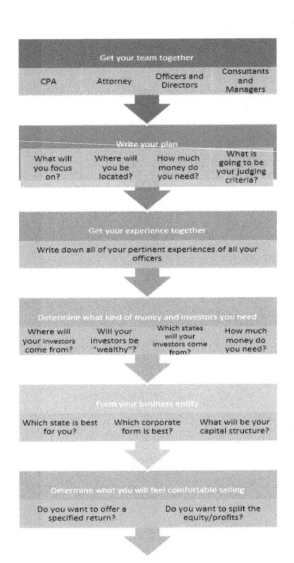

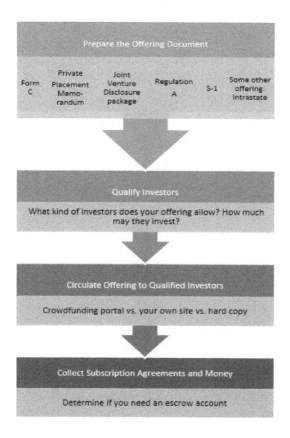

Being fully prepared is of the utmost importance. Your campaign will be stopped dead in its tracks by the SEC, the investors, or the portal if you don't have everything done properly.

"We rejected an issuer from our portal due to the issuer not being ready for a proper and successful campaign. The client had not followed Finaeos 'Built for Equity' program properly, which resulted in not passing our compliance and we stopped moving forward with the campaign." states Robert Gerrard, COO of Finaeos.

"Our 'Built for Equity' program has an established process and documentation requirements before a crowdfunding campaign can be achieved. The process is designed to weed out those who are not ready, which was the case in this situation."

Like many other crowdfunding portals, Patch of Land, Inc. conducted their own crowdfunding campaign on SeedInvest.com. Their success was directly attributed to their preparedness. Amy Wan shares, "We had our ducks in a row with technology, financials, legal, and disclosures. We were also willing to put in the elbow grease to get it done. Many people think crowdfunding is a 'post it and see what happens' deal, but in fact, you have to work really hard--as hard if not harder than the portal--to get to the finish line. It is important to provide transparency and access to your investors. Our executive team was not just a digital resume, but very interactive in the process. We made videos introducing each executive. Every executive did what was necessary to insure success, including in-person meetings or phone calls, to get the deals done." Patch of Land was very successful in taking this approach and raised $2.4 million on Seed Invest.

Following this chapter, specifically, will put your campaign on track to success towards acceptance by a crowdfunding portal for funding.

# XII.   THE RIGHT TEAM

*"Individual commitment to a group effort - that is what
makes a team work, a company work, a society work, a
civilization work."*
Vince Lombardi

In raising capital, you need to have the right
team, both internally and externally. Your internal
management team has to know what they are
doing and must be able to convey the proper
message. This can all be assisted by the external
team:

1.  Securities Attorney (if you are launching
    a securities-based campaign)

2.  CPA (possibly an auditor if you are
    conducting a Regulation A filing).

3.  Crowdfunding Portal – if you choose to

crowdfund through an established portal.

4.  Marketing Team – you need this whether you are conducting a product based or securities based campaign.

5.  Technology team – this may be your crowdfunding portal. If you are choosing to crowdfund through your own site, you will need the proper technology to do it right. You will need this not just for the fundraising portion, but also for the ongoing reporting and care of your investors.

Scott Purcell, CEO of FundAmerica.com attributes much of the success of Elio Motors' Regulation A offering to the entire team. Elio Motors, the first Regulation A+ offering since the rule changes in June 2015, launched in November 2015 and hit their minimum requirement of $12 million within 5 days of launch. It went on to raise millions more before successfully closing.

"[Elio Motors] had a great technology and back-office services provider, of course! Seriously, they did a great job of marketing. The platform they used, StartEngine.com, was instrumental in helping them get the word out and stay organized." Scott and his team provided the technology to get the investors in the door and helped them clear investors. "Our Invest Now transaction engine was used to enable investors to invest in the offering. We then cleared funds into escrow, performed AML and provided all back office services."

Putting the team together is one thing, but it is also important to be mindful of Chapter 0. Thinking out and planning your offering is imperative. You need to bring the team the tools necessary to be successful. Robert Gerrard, COO of Finaeos encourages potential crowdfunding companies to "be prepared to dedicate the money, time and resources to do things correctly and prepare for 'Build for Equity.' Investors will reward those candidates who do, with a successful equity crowdfunded campaign."

*Provide the team with what they need*
*Find the right portal for your campaign*

Amy Wan is Chief Legal Counsel of PatchofLand.com. Patch of Land only seeks out opportunities to which they can be of a value. She highly suggests you only search out a platform that values your offer. "When working with a platform to raise capital, ensure that the platform is providing you support. Make sure they're going to do more than just list your campaign. Anyone can do that, but a good platform should make real efforts to make sure your campaign is successful. They should care about quality, not just quantity, of those using their platform."

Henry Chavez is an Audit Manager with Spiegel Accountancy. Their firm has experience with handling the audit and accounting needs of a variety of companies from really small private companies to large publicly traded companies. "Our recommendation when considering setting up a new crowd funding platform is to consult with your team of legal and accounting professionals to ensure your structure and operating platform is compliant with regulations and will accomplish the financial objectives of the investors and fund manager." Henry recommends.

"Crowd funders will generally register with the SEC through either a Regulation A+ or public filing registration. This is common to allow the fund manager to attract non-accredited investors rather than be limited to only accredited investors. Careful thought should be given to which registration is appropriate considering the level of compliance regulations they create."

### *Marketing, Marketing, Marketing*

As this book has discussed time and time again, throwing a campaign up on a portal is useless. For those potential clients that come to my firm looking to conduct a Regulation A offering, I will not let them proceed without a marketing plan and budget.

Investors, like any customer, must be swooned. If you don't have an internal, proficient marketing team, then be sure to look for one externally prior to launching any campaign.

### Take care of the tribe

Whether you are taking on investors or customers, it is absolutely imperative that you care for the "tribe." In the case of investors, it is also legally imperative.

Craig Delinger with Crowdfund CPA specializes in auditing and accounting requirements for crowdfunding companies. There is a requirement for crowdfunding companies, or any capital raising company for that matter, to provide ongoing reporting to their investors. "I consider the most important aspect of an offering under SEC rules to be ensuring you provide investors with complete and reliable information to base their investment decision upon. Companies utilizing Regulation A need to step back and put themselves in potential investors' shoes and consider what information about where the company is and where it is going is important to the investment decision, and likewise, what terms, investor protections, and policies the company can put in place to alleviate those concerns. Every founder/CEO would prefer to retain exclusive voting powers, give up as little of their company as possible, and reduce regulatory and reporting burdens, but these are crucial aspects of the investment decision that could sway an otherwise interested investor. Not having an appropriate governance structure, overvaluing the company via share price, or retaining too large of an interest in your company and not committing to regular, consistent, and ongoing reporting could be negative signals to an investor. Conversely, companies can enhance both the marketability and valuation of their offering by providing investors with risk mitigating safeguards. For instance, an investor would be more likely to invest in, and at a higher valuation, a company with an active board of outside investors, voting rights for incoming investors, corporate governance dictating consistent, reliable, and timely financial reporting, as opposed to a company without such safeguards. While investors' needs vary depending on the nature of the company, a value/cost analysis should be performed in structuring a company and offering to ensure the appropriate balance is struck for the circumstances."

Phew! That's a lot. So what should you do about? Well, first and foremost, enlist the services of a quality securities attorney to assist you with the initial disclosure. Second, do what you say you are going to do in the documents you provide to the investors. This includes ongoing reporting to them. Investors are going to want to know how their investment is doing, what the crowdfunding company is planning next, and what the financial status of the crowdfunding company is.

To this end, I normally recommend quarterly reporting to your investors. I also recommend a well- developed newsletter, not just for your current investors and customers, but for those potential investors and customers. If you go to our website at TheCrowdfundingMyth.com and sign up for our mailing list, we will provide you with some great resources on reporting and effective newsletter campaigns.

### *I feel like there is more*

Well, there is. That's why the team is so very important. You need to work on your business, implementing the plan, and growing it – this is why you hire the team to help you with corporate structure (securities attorney), auditing and accounting (CPA/auditor), taxes and distributions to your investors (CPA), offering documents and structure (securities attorney), marketing (marketing team and crowdfunding portal), fundraising (crowdfunding portal and technology), and reporting to your investors (assisted by your CPA and technology.) Use the multitude of resources in this book. Go to our website to find even more resources to help you with your campaign like additional crowdfunding portals,

CPA's, marketing gurus, templates, FAQ's, videos, and more. I will have even more stories, successes, failures, and examples for you to enjoy and learn from.

Finally, if you really feel stuck, email us! I would love to hear from you and what you thought of this book – info@crowdfundingmyth. If you tell me what you think of the book by giving it a review on Amazon, I will even send you a free business plan template.

YOU CAN DO THIS! Now go fund something.

## ABOUT THE AUTHOR

**Jillian Sidoti**, Esq. is one of the country's leading experts on Regulation A+. Since 2008, Jillian has submitted multiple Regulation A Offering Circulars to the Securities Exchange Commission for approval making her one of the few attorneys familiar with the law prior to the changes under the JOBS Act. Since the JOBS Act, Jillian has assisted multiple companies and entrepreneurs realize their fundraising goals through Crowdfunding, 506©, and Regulation A. She is a practiced speaker whose engagements are well attended and often come to produce sound bites and additional discourse. In *Crowdfunding Myth*, Jillian enumerates on the falsehoods that people tend to believe about crowdfunding and points prospective business owners in the right direction. Prior to her legal career, Jillian owned and operated a record label enabling her to tour worldwide with artists, including visiting South Africa, Canada, Europe, and the United States. Using that experience, Jillian has been commissioned to write articles and contracts for many music industry entities. For several years, Jillian taught Finance and Accounting for the BS and MBA programs at the University of Redlands, drawing on her experience as Financial Analyst, Controller, and CFO for many companies from manufacturing to real estate development. Jillian also taught a Small Business Management class where students are taught the anatomy of a business plan.

Jillian is currently a partner in the firm Trowbridge Taylor Sidoti – a securities boutique law firm with offices in southern California and Florida. They can be found on the web at SyndicationLawyers.com

Jillian has three amazing little boys Tyler, Tommy, and Nikola and an amazing husband, Derek.

---

[i] http://www.getrichslowly.org/blog/2015/03/05/the-rise-of-alternative-investments/

[ii] http://money.cnn.com/2016/01/12/investing/stocks-lose-1-trillion-2016/

[iii] http://www.nasdaq.com/article/americans-have-relatively-poor-net-wealth-cm257517

---

iv

http://www.forbes.com/sites/moneywisewomen/2
012/03/21/average-america-vs-the-one-
percent/#5dae323e11a8